Knitting
Stylish Stuff
from Your Stash

20 Scrappy Designs

Erica Berntsen

Landauer Publishing

Knitting Stylish Stuff from Your Stash

© Erica Berntsen
First published by Kagge Forlag, 2024
Published in agreement with Oslo Literary Agency

English translation, *Knitting Stylish Stuff from Your Stash*, © 2025 Fox Chapel Publishing Company

Knitting Stylish Stuff from Your Stash is an translation of the 2024 version originally published in Norwegian by Kagge Forlag under the title *Bernt. Strikk Med Restegarn* in Oslo, Norway. This version is published by Landauer, an imprint of Fox Chapel Publishing Company, Inc.

Project Team
Managing Editor: Gretchen Bacon
Acquisitions Editor: Amelia Johanson
Tech Editor: Rita Greenfeder
Editor: Christa Oestreich
Designer: Freire Disseny + Comunicació
Indexer: Jay Kreider

ISBN 978-1-63981-121-2

Library of Congress Control Number: 2024945984

To learn more about the other great books from Fox Chapel Publishing, or to find a retailer near you, call toll-free 800-457-9112, send mail to
903 Square Street,
Mount Joy, PA 17552,
or visit us at www.FoxChapelPublishing.com.

We are always looking for talented authors. To submit an idea, please send a brief inquiry to acquisitions@foxchapelpublishing.com.

Printed in China
First printing

Contents

Coming to Terms with My Yarn Consumption

In December 2022, I decided to clean out my yarn stash. I was moving to a much smaller apartment soon and needed to get an overview of what I had stocked up. Also, this was the day before an exam, and since my procrastination gene is strong, there was no doubt that this was a good time to do anything but prepare for the exam. "How long can it take?" I thought.

Four hours later, I had cleared, sorted, and distributed all my yarn into ten brand new projects. Ten! And it wasn't just mittens and small pieces, but large, chunky knitwear. The amount of yarn was overwhelming, and I was a little embarrassed. This was not very sustainable.

This was the start of my Zero Waste collection, which quickly gained a lot of attention. It turned out that there were many people who recognized themselves in my situation of large amounts of yarn piling up. In a survey carried out by the leftover yarn app SaveYarn, 43% of knitters said they had over 100 skeins sitting at home. On a popular secondhand market, there are over 15,000 yarn listings—with an average of 18 skeins per ad*—which means there are over 270,000 skeins of yarn for sale. If you estimate an average of 15 skeins used for a sweater, that amounts to 18,000 sweaters. That is so many leftover yarn projects!

There are huge amounts of yarn out there, and I get the impression that most people know what to do with all their yarn or where to start. This book can help you get you on the path of rethinking leftover yarn, making knitting a breeze and making it even easier to slim down your yarn stash once and for all. I want to show that knitting with leftover yarn can be at least as fun as buying new yarn—if not even more fun!

---

*   *The average is calculated from the first 100 ads that came up when I searched for yarn on Finn.no, calculated on 9/25/2023. The estimate is based on 1 skein generally considered to be 1.8oz (50g).*

DO I NEED LEFTOVER YARN FOR THIS BOOK?

The main message in this book is: Use the yarn you have before buying new. Of course, I hope to inspire as many people as possible to use their leftovers, but that does not mean that my patterns can only be knitted with leftover yarn. If you don't have leftovers lying around, there is of course no shame in buying new ones.

If you have leftovers lying around, but not enough to knit an entire sweater, you can also buy more yarn to supplement. The patterns in the book often have a base color and a rest color, or pattern color. If you don't have enough yarn, you can, for example, buy the base color and use the rest for what is to be knitted in other colors. For example, if you buy half of the yarn for a sweater, you can use leftovers for the other half, and any use of leftovers is better than nothing.

But if you are going to buy yarn first, I encourage you to also check out a secondhand market before you run to a yarn store. Or ask a fiend, and maybe you can help another knitter slim down their yarn stash.

RIGHT: Use up all those yarns you bought but don't have a project for and those leftovers that can't complete a piece to make bold, beautiful sweaters you'll treasure.

Five Good Reasons to Knit with Leftover Yarn

1. IT'S MORE SUSTAINABLE

Knitting is part of the slow-fashion movement—a sustainable alternative to the fast-fashion industry, which is often characterized by a fast pace and poor-quality materials. If you knit with good-quality yarn, you get garments that can last for generations. But having enough yarn in your stash for 10 sweaters is not very sustainable. A sustainable lifestyle means using what you have, and that also applies to yarn! Although small-batch yarn is the most sustainable, a great alternative is to use up what we already have.

2. IT'S MORE ECONOMIC

To be completely honest, part of my motivation for starting this project was financial. Good-quality yarn can be expensive, and as a student when first conceiving this project, I couldn't afford to buy new yarn. When I decided to clean out my yarn stash, I realized that it was almost like going yarn shopping, only everything was free. So collect all your yarn in one place and see it in a new light— suddenly you can conjure up the most beautiful garments without sacrificing your wallet!

3. YOU CAN TAKE BIGGER CHANCES

When using the yarn you already have, it's as if the threshold for trying things out is a little lower. After all, you have invested nothing but time in the project, and you didn't waste money if it doesn't go the way you planned. My projects don't always turn out the way I planned, but when I first dared to take a few chances and follow my gut feeling, the result was usually even better than I had originally imagined!

4. LEFTOVERS MAKE UNIQUE GARMENTS

Knitting with leftover yarn forces you to use your creativity, and you have to make some choices along the way: maybe you run out of a color or a type of yarn and have to switch to something else, maybe you have to adjust the length of the garment to get enough yarn or to use up all the yarn. Dare to make these choices, and I promise you that the result will be a completely unique sweater.

5. KNIT WITH A GOOD CONSCIENCE

When you knit with leftover yarn, you can have a better conscience for both your wallet and the environment. Take bigger chances and let your creativity flourish. What's the worst that could happen? Fortunately, knitting is recyclable, so if the result isn't quite what you thought it would be, you can always unravel it and try again (and although it can of course be time-consuming and a bit demotivating to "frog," it's always worth it in the end!). So what are you waiting for? Pull out the leftover yarn and knit with a clear conscience!

You already love the yarn in your stash—that's why you bought it! Now it's time to find an excuse to use it.

Leftover Yarn vs. Yarn from Your Stash

In this book, I use the terms leftover yarn and yarn stash interchangeably. Therefore, I think it might be a good idea to define what I mean when I talk about the two.

I define **leftover yarn** as yarn left over after a finished project. It can be both started and whole skeins. Leftover yarn can be characterized by the fact that you have smaller quantities of each yarn weight or color, and you are often dependent on putting together different yarn weights and colors to get enough yarn for an entire project.

Yarn from your stash can contain leftover yarn, but it can also contain yarn that you bought and never used for whatever reason. The yarn stash is therefore all the yarn you have lying around. Your yarn stash may also contain knitted sweaters that didn't turn out quite as you had imagined or that

LEFT: Along with helping you feel good about using up your unused yarn, these sweaters also just look good!

are never used—don't forget that there is great value in the knitted garments that are collecting dust in the wardrobe!

NEW YARN, SECONDHAND YARN, AND USED YARN

New yarn is yarn that has not been owned by anyone before, which comes directly from the yarn manufacturer or store. **Secondhand yarn** can be brand-new skeins that have never been used before but are characterized as yarn that has been owned by someone else before you, which you have either bought privately or received. **Used yarn**, also called destash, is yarn that already has been knitted with, but it is stretched so that it can be used again.

Knitting Responsibly

In the old days, people knitted because it was the only way to get clothes that kept you warm in the winter. Today it is cheaper and saves time to buy a knitted sweater from the store. We live in a fast-fashion society, and generally in a society where everything must happen at a breakneck pace. Therefore, we often need to calm down, use our hands, and relax. Knitting has gone from being absolutely necessary to survive the cold winter to becoming a luxury that gives us mindfulness in a hectic everyday life. In many ways, we find ourselves in a time where we need knitting more than we need knitwear.

In addition, buying new yarn is easier than before. It is said that knitting is two hobbies: buying yarn and knitting with it. Walking into a yarn shop is like walking into a sweet shop, it's full of beautiful colors and textures—it's easy to get tempted! Since we no longer knit to survive, one can easily forget that the result of the knitted garment must also have a useful value. Completing a knitting project is not as much fun as starting anew, and you can quickly be bitten by planning sickness.* The result of this illness was, for my part, a pile of unfinished projects, also called UFOs. These UFOs eventually became fertile ground for a lot of bad choices.

Today, we are bombarded on social media with images of new projects and finished knitted garments that give the impression that knitted garments are being produced at a fast pace. There is always something new about trends: new colors, shapes, structures, and patterns. And the list of knitted garments you want is long! But sustainable knitting is also about knitting a garment that have value, which is used until someone else can take the garment when you no longer need it.

---

* **Planning sickness:** *A term used in the knitting world when you want to knit many different things and therefore start several projects at the same time.*

RIGHT: By making garments you love and that will last, you're not only helping yourself—you're also helping slow down fast fashion.

WE NEED TO TALK ABOUT UNRAVELING

I know this might be like swearing in church, but we need to talk about unraveling unused or unfinished projects. You know that sweater you knitted that didn't fit as well as you thought, which is now gathering dust in the wardrobe—the garment that has a yarn value of a few dozen or maybe over a hundred dollars? Or that sweater with a small mistake on it, or maybe the knitting tension wasn't quite right so it's too big or too small, or that project you can never find enough motivation to finish? Maybe you don't recognize yourself in any of these examples, but if you do, we need to have a chat about unraveling. Is it really that dangerous?

Unraveling is in many ways the most boring activity I can think of. Hours of work right in the sink! But it's also the best activity because it gives me the opportunity to try again. Knitwear is, after all, recyclable—so maybe it's time to go yarn shopping in your own wardrobe.

All the time, I see knitters selling their knitted garments at a price that is often much lower than the yarn value. I've been there myself, but now I've started sorting out these garments and unfinished projects to reuse the yarn. For example, the Cables and Coffee Sweater is knitted from an unused striped mohair sweater that I unraveled and then repurposed the colors from the various stripes again. Before you sell your unused sweater for a bargain, do some research—can you reuse this yarn instead of buying more?

The striped sections on this sweater came from a previous project.

Colors

I am not an expert in color theory; I usually work with color based on personal experience. This experience has been built up over time with a lot of trial and error.
I have tried my hand at different color combinations and unraveled countless times when the garment did not turn out as I had intended. But I'll do my best to share what I've learned along the way, so you hopefully don't have to spend as much time making mistakes like I did.

COLOR CATEGORIES

I always sort colors by earth tones, vibrant colors, pastel colors, and neutral colors. The **earth tones** are brown, moss green, gray, and copper colored and are often in darker shades. These usually go well with each other, and I rarely combine them with other color categories, except for the neutral colors. **Pastel colors** are colors in light shades, often pink, purple, yellow, or blue. Pastel colors go extremely well with each other and with white. You can also use pastel colors to tone down vibrant colors. **Vibrant colors** have saturation, meaning the color is not "watered down" with white or black. These therefore do well as contrast with lighter or less vibrant colors. The **neutral colors** are, as the name suggests, neutral; they consist of white and black along with shades of beige and gray, among other colors.

On page 20 are color combinations that are based on what I found in my yarn stash, but you are welcome to create your own categories and palettes if you do not feel that my examples suit your starting point. These palettes are only examples to make it easier to visualize and plan which colors you can put together. The categories are also not conclusive on which colors go together and which do not.

RIGHT: A bold look for your garment can be achieved by combining vibrant and pastel colors.

Examples of Earth Tones

Examples of Pastels

Examples of Vibrant Colors

Examples of Neutrals

HOW TO PUT COLORS TOGETHER

BASE COLOR

A base color repeats itself frequently throughout the garment. Most of the patterns in this book use a base color, either as one of several threads being used or as part of a pattern. The base color is the canvas for the knitwear and the color that brings the rest of the colors together. If you have a lot of one color in your yarn stash, it can act as your base—if not, you can buy a base color that unites the rest of your colors.

Choose a color that is in the same palette as the rest, or choose a contrasting color that can mix several color categories into one. The base color does not have to be a solid color either, but it should be roughly the same shade as the other colors. Also note that the thicker the thread you use as a base color, the clearer and more dominant the color will be.

ACCENT COLOR

In some of the projects in this book, I refer to an accent color in addition to the base color. The accent color, in contrast to the base color, can combine several different colors and accents in whatever amount you desire. The term accent color is an attempt to convey that these yarns are used in smaller amounts but are no less prominent. Remember that even if a project consists of both a base color and an accent color, you can always replace the base color with an accent color and vice versa.

EXAMPLE: STARRY NIGHT CARDIGAN

In this project, I used vibrant blue thick mohair as the base color. In addition, I used countless small scraps as accent colors, in both vibrant and pastel colors. The color blue is dominant and ties together the rest of the colors, which alone might not have gone together as well.

USING VIBRANT COLORS AS A BASE

Saturated colors make for an excellent base. When you choose a vibrant color for the base color, this will drown out less vibrant colors in the knitwear, and you can thus combine several accent colors without it getting too messy—after all, the biggest contrast comes from the vibrant base color.

DARK AND LIGHT COLORS

When putting colors together, you may want to think about the effect dark and light colors will have on the overall design. For example, if you knit with light colors and switch to a dark color, this transition will be very clear, and the dark color will contrast with the light. This can create a cool effect, but it can also be stark and disjointed if you don't have a plan.

If you have mostly light yarn and a few leftovers in dark, it may be a good idea to split up the dark leftovers and distribute them over the project so that the effect is consistent. If you have about the same amount of dark and light or vibrant and neutral colors, you can also try a gradient, where you go from light to dark, from vibrant colors to neutral, or vice versa on both.

EXAMPLE: CABLES AND COFFEE SWEATER

This sweater is knitted with thick mohair in light pink, white, and powder pink as the base color, and with colorful scraps in a thick mohair for the accent. Here I had both vibrant colors, pastel colors, and a neutral color (white), but I saw that the dark purple stood out even more than the others. Therefore, I divided this color into many small skeins. This way, the stripe with purple was not too thick or dominant in the garment.

CONCRETE TECHNIQUES FOR COLORFUL KNITTING

PLAYING WITH COLOR

When I knit with different colors, I like to disperse them over the whole knitwear so that I get a nice distribution. Playing with color is well suited to patterns where several threads are knitted at a time, or where a pattern has not been established already. This can create a pattern that looks less rigid, using your color palette in a more original and artistic way.

Playing with color is great if you have small skeins that you want to use up, and if you have larger skeins, these can be split into smaller skeins to achieve the same effect of colors strewn about the garment. This distribution can be knitted with a base color for a more grounded look, or it can be knitted with different colors alternating throughout for a more chaotic, cool, and playful effect.

You can achieve this effect in two different ways:

Feel It Out as You Go

Start with one color and knit as long as you want. Stop at a random place and cut the thread. Switch to the next color. Get a feel for how wide you want the stripes to be in the different colors, and how much you want each color to stand out. Make sure you have enough yarn in the different colors for each part of the garment. This way of knitting gives you more control, in that you can decide how much you want to knit with each color, but it also gives you choices to adapt or experiment along the way.

Let Your Stash Decide

Divide larger skeins into smaller skeins of different sizes before you start knitting. If you have a lot of one color, for example, you can create larger skeins in this color; however, if you have a color that stands out, you can split this color into smaller skeins so it's not too dominant along the way. Distribute the different skeins around the garment: If you are knitting a sweater, for example, you will need the most skeins for the torso, but also a couple for the sleeves and neck, so make sure you have a few skeins in each color for each part. Try your hand at the order of the colors and let the different sizes of the skeins control the result.

It was about here when I realized I didn't have enough pink for the rest of the Streetwear Sweater. Because I switched to white, this garment became an eye-catcher!

GRADIENTS

Gradients, or ombres, can be knitted to make the transition between two colors more fluid. For example, this technique can be used if you are going to

- change from one color to another (Sunset Over the City Sweater, page 46)

- switch from vibrant or dark colors to neutral or light colors, or vice versa (Streetwear Sweater, page 134)

These steps demonstrate a gradual transition between two colors (labeled A and B) that can be used for any project you like. If you want a shorter gradient, you can skip straight to step 3 or step 5.

Knit with Color A up to where you want to start the gradient:

Step 1: Knit 1 round with Color B.

Step 2: Knit 7 rounds with Color A.

Step 3: Knit 1 round with Color B.

Step 4: Knit 5 rounds with Color A.

Step 5: Knit 1 round with Color B.

Step 6: Knit 3 rounds with Color A.

Step 7: Knit 1 round with Color B.

Step 8: Knit every other round with Color A and Color B. When you run out of Color A, continue with Color B on both rounds.

RIGHT: Sunset Over the City Sweater uses a shorter gradient at the bottom while the rest remains one color.

Tension and Gauge

When you knit with leftover yarn, the first and perhaps most important step is checking the gauge. The knitting gauge tells you what dimensions the stitch count will give you. If your gauge does not match the project, it can have a big impact on the size of the garment. The greater the deviation in tension, the greater the deviation from the measurements in the project will be on the finished garment. However, your gauges don't have to agree with the gauges stated in this book, but it is important to know how the tension affects the result.

HOW TO MAKE A GAUGE

Knit a test swatch with the yarn in your project before you start knitting the garment. Each of the patterns in this book has a separate instruction for knitting a sample swatch measuring 4¾" x 4¾" (12.1 x 12.1cm). When you have knitted this gauge, measure 4" x 4" (10.2 x 10.2cm) on the center and count how many stitches are within the 4" (10.2cm) width and height. **Note:** Hang onto the gauges you knit, as they can be used in the Patchwork Cardigan or Patchwork Tote Bag.

LEFT: Hang onto your gauges! They can be reused to make a Patchwork Cardigan or Tote Bag.

TIP

Some people knit tighter or looser when they knit in rows rather than in the round. Therefore, the gauge tension varies slightly from the knitwear itself. Feel free to check the knitting tension along the way if you want to be completely sure it matches the project.

IF THE TENSION IS TOO LOOSE

If you have fewer stitches on your gauge than stated in the instructions, the tension is too loose. The garment will therefore be larger than the size given.

Example: If the gauge in the project states 16 stitches = 4" (10.2cm), and you have 15 stitches = 4" (10.2cm), a stitch count of 200 stitches will give 52¾" (134cm) instead of 49¼" (125.1cm), so the sweater will be almost 4" (10.2cm) larger.

When the knitting tension is too loose, you have two choices:

1. Go down another full needle size until the gauge is correct.
2. Continue knitting with the tension you have, but consider going down a clothing size or two to get the measurements you want.

IF THE TENSION IS TOO TIGHT

If you have more stitches on your gauge than stated in the instructions, the tension is too tight. The garment will therefore be smaller than the size given.

Example: If the gauge in the project states 16 stitches = 4" (10.2cm), and you have 17 stitches = 4" (10.2cm), a stitch count of 200 stitches will give 46½" (118.1cm) instead of 49¼" (125.1cm), so the sweater will be almost 3" (7.6cm) smaller.

When the knitting tension is too tight, you have two choices:

1. Go up a full needle size until the gauge is correct.
2. Continue knitting with the tension you have, but consider going up a clothing size or two to get the measurements you want.

RIGHT: Gauges are important for ensuring that your garment will turn out at the correct size. This is especially important for sweaters and other things you will wear.

GAUGE EQUATION

The knitting gauge can be used for more than making sure that the measurements on the garment will match. It can also be used to find the correct number of stitches based on how many inches (centimeters) you want, or how many inches (centimeters) a given number of stitches will give. The equations below show you how you can use the gauge to calculate your own sizes, and thus assemble and create your very own leftover yarn designs.

HOW TO CALCULATE THE NUMBER OF STITCHES

$$\frac{desired\ number\ of\ inches \times gauge\ stitches}{4} = stitches$$

$$\frac{desired\ number\ of\ cm \times gauge\ stitches}{10} = stitches$$

EXAMPLE:

You have a gauge with 16 stitches = 4" (10.2cm) and want a sweater that has a circumference of 48" (121.9cm). The gauge equation will then look like this:

$$\frac{48 \times 16}{4} = 192\ sts$$

Then you know that to get 48" (121.9cm) in circumference, you must have 192 stitches in the torso.

HOW TO CALCULATE THE LENGTH

$$\left(\frac{stitches}{gauge\ stitches} \right) \times 4 = number\ of\ inches$$

$$\left(\frac{stitches}{gauge\ stitches} \right) \times 10 = number\ of\ cm$$

EXAMPLE:

You have a stitch count of 201 stitches and a gauge with 15 stitches = 4" (10.2cm). The gauge equation will then look like this:

$$\left(\frac{201}{15} \right) \times 4 = 53\ \tfrac{1}{2}"$$

Then you know that if you have a stitch count of 204 stitches and a gauge with 15 stitches, the piece will measure 53 ½" (135.9cm).

LEFT: If desired, you can wash your gauge swatch to have a better idea of how much your sweater will shrink or stretch.

Tools and Techniques

GEAR I SWEAR BY

There is an incredible number of knitting tools, materials, and notions on the market with different functions. Here I have collected the ones I swear by, which I have used diligently while making the yarn-stash projects.

CIRCULAR NEEDLES

Circular knitting needles stand out because they are connected by a cord. This cord is a long silicone thread that you can attach to the needle and keep your stitches on. You can easily slip the stitches on and off the cord without having to thread each stitch onto a needle. I use it when I let stitches rest during a project, or if I want to try on a garment while still knitting but prevent the stitches from falling off the needle.

STITCH MARKERS

Stitch markers are a knitter's best friend because they keep track of where you are in a project. In addition, there are now countless varieties of these notions, which can also decorate the knitwear as jewelry. For the patterns in this book, I often use stitch markers to mark when the round starts, when I am halfway through the work, and where stitches should be increased or decreased.

Stitch markers are not very expensive and are a good investment to make knitting easier. If you don't have stitch markers, you can easily make your own by tying a thread into a small loop that you can put on the needle.

YARN BASKET AND PROJECT BAGS

When I divide my yarn into different projects, I always use project bags to keep track of everything. My storage options can be anything from cloth bags with elastic to tote bags to plastic bags—I use what I have on hand. When actually starting a new project, I collect all the skeins I'm going to use in a yarn basket. Because everything is gathered in one place, I can easily find it and put it away.

Knitting leftover yarn can be chaotic, so it is important to have good systems for your various projects. I always have an empty tote bag or project bag laying around, so I can easily pack a project and take it with me.

MAKE FLAT YARN BALLS

This technique popped up in my social media when I was about halfway through my yarn-stash project, and I've been swearing by it ever since. It is perfect when you have unraveled a sweater or split a skein. When using this technique, you get compact balls where you can also find the end of the yarn on the inside, and thus be able to knit with two threads at the same time. It's easier to knit with these yarn balls than the round ones you usually get, which always roll away.

Step 1: Place the thread on the palm of your hand.

Step 2: Wrap the thread around your hand at a 45 degree angle.

Step 3: When your hand starts to get full, move the yarn about 1" (2.5cm) to the left.

Step 4: Continue wrapping the thread around your hand at the same angle, and repeat step 3 as often as necessary.

Step 5: When you run out of yarn, thread the ball by hand and voilà! You have a flat ball where you can pick up the yarn end at both ends.

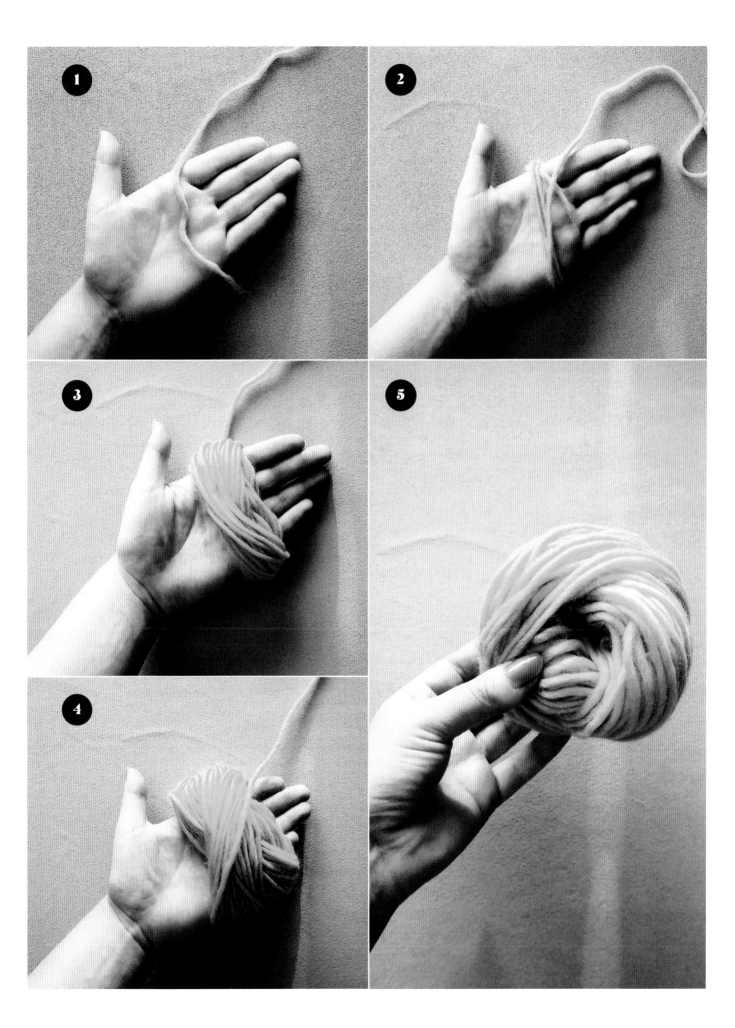

JOINING THREADS

With leftover-yarn knitting, there is a lot of reattaching threads. If I'm honest, this is a step I often put off as long as I can. But here are my best techniques to make joining a little faster:

KNOTS

Using knots to attach threads is a bit of a controversial technique. Still, I have good experience with using knots, especially in leftover-yarn projects where the color and thread change often. Knots are a nice technique to use as long as the knots are on the inside of the sweater where they are not visible or in the way. Double- or triple-knot the threads so you are sure they are tight. Although the knots are usually enough to hold the yarn ends in place over time, I tend to leave a bit of yarn at the ends of the knots, so I can go back and secure them with a crochet hook to make sure they stay in place.

Be aware that not all projects are suitable for knots. The thicker your yarn, the thicker and more noticeable the knots will be. If your garment will sit close to the skin, like the Streetwear Mittens (page 148), the knots will be very noticeable. If the yarn is very smooth, such as cotton yarn, the knots are also more likely to unravel. Then it might be trickier to attach the threads in a different way.

WEAVE IN AS YOU GO

When it is not suitable to use knots, you can weave the thread in while working. Add new yarn a couple of stitches before you run out of a skein, and knit two to three stitches with the doubled thread. Now you have knitted the thread in and are ready to continue with this new yarn. The transition is so small that it won't be noticeable, but be aware that the thicker your thread, the more visible the transition will be.

USE A CROCHET HOOK

Using a crochet hook to attach threads is a lifehack that made the process so much easier for me. I learned early in the leftover-yarn project that the best way to attach threads when you've finished the garment is to use a crochet hook. Thread the crochet hook through the stitches on the inside of the garment, pick up the thread, and pull it through. Feel free to thread it through two stitches at a time in a zigzag pattern, so you are absolutely sure that it fits well.

Yarn Amount

Knitting with leftover yarn is not an exact science. Since different types of yarn in the same category can have different running lengths, it can be difficult to calculate the exact amount of yarn needed. The amount of yarn indicated in each project is therefore only a suggestion, but it can give an idea of how much yarn you need. Not sure if you have enough yarn for a project? Then there are several ways to proceed.

OPTIMIZE YOUR YARN

If you are knitting a top-down garment, it may be a good idea to knit the neck and sleeves before completing the torso. This way, you can more easily see how much yarn you have left when you get to the torso, and how far your yarn will go. If the sweater is knitted from the bottom up, you can start by knitting the sleeves first before starting the torso, so that you can adjust the length of the torso if you have too little yarn or have plenty of yarn left over.

EXAMPLE:

On the Streetwear Sweater, I was unsure whether I would have enough yarn in the colors I wanted. I started knitting the front and back, then the neck and sleeves. Once the neck was knitted and the sleeves started, I divided the remaining skeins of scraps into three parts: one for each of the sleeves and one for the torso. This way, I knew that I was going to have approximately the same amount of yarn for each section.

When I started to run out of colorful scraps, I knitted gradients and switched to a neutral color on the bottom of the torso and sleeves. This way, I got enough yarn to complete the project, and the sweater got a cool and complete ombre effect.

RIGHT: The gradient on the Streetwear Sweater was because I nearly ran out of my colorful scraps. Now I wouldn't change a thing!

WHAT IF YOU RUN OUT OF YARN?

My very best tip for calculating the amount of yarn you need is to just get started. Start knitting, and if you run out of yarn, it's not the end of the world. Instead, it might lead to a choice that gives your garment a completely unique, creative, and fresh look.

There are four options if you run out of yarn:

OPTION 1: CHECK YOUR STASH

Always start by taking a look around your yarn stash. Do you have something that could work as an alternative? A different color or maybe even a different weight? Also look in your wardrobe or UFO pile—do you have any garments you never wear or projects that were never completed, where the yarn could be more suitable for this project?

OPTION 2: ASK A FRIEND

If you are looking for a specific type of yarn or color, you can always consult a knitter friend or family. See if they have any leftovers laying around that you can get or exchange for.

OPTION 3: BUY ON A SECONDHAND MARKET

As mentioned at the beginning of the book, there are enormous quantities of leftover yarn on secondhand markets. You might even find the exact type you are looking for at a slightly cheaper price! For example, Etsy and eBay are great for buying and selling leftover yarn.

OPTION 4: BUY NEW

There is no shame in buying new yarn. If you end up buying a couple of skeins, you've still saved the environment and your wallet with the skeins you used from your own stash! If you buy new first, remember to choose good materials that will last a long time, and not buy more than you need.

Don't forget that the vast majority of yarn shops also exchange unopened skeins. If you have any laying around, it doesn't hurt to bring your skeins along and ask if you can trade them in for something new.

TIP

Swap nights are very popular when it comes to clothes. Why not organize a swap night for leftover yarn? Ask your friends to bring the leftover yarn they never get to use, and collect it all in one place. One knitter's leftovers are another knitter's treasure trove! When the exchange is over, you can knit and enjoy yourself together like on a regular knitting evening.

Ask your friends if they
have extra yarn you can
use, or do a yarn swap!

Get Started with a Leftover Yarn Project

OVERVIEW

I get the impression that there are many people who want to use their leftover yarn, but don't know where to start. Therefore, I created a step-by-step method that gives you an overview of your stash and the means to sort it so it's more manageable for new projects. This method works for me and my yarn stash and has resulted in a total of 20 leftover yarn garments. I've gone through the process several times along the way, and it works just as well for each one. Hopefully it works as well for you and your yarn stash as it did for me!

SORT

The first thing you should do when you start knitting leftover yarn is to get an overview of your yarn stash. Set aside some time, collect all the yarn in one place, and spread it out.

Now you can start sorting. This process can make it easier to visualize how much yarn you have and which projects the yarn can be used for; also, it can help you plan future leftover yarn projects. I use four steps when sorting my yarn stash.

STEP 1: YARN WEIGHTS

Sort the yarn by weight. Feel free to weigh how much yarn you have of the various yarn weights, and write it down in a notebook, on a spreadsheet, or wherever you prefer. There are also several good apps out there that can help you keep track of your stash (for example, the KNIT app).

STEP 2: YARN CATEGORIES

Once broken down by weight, sort the yarn into different yarn categories. The categories can be based on anything from quality to material to knitting firmness, with a little wiggle room in each. For example, a mohair has a different texture than a cotton yarn, so you might want to separate them. However, if a thick mohair yarn has the same gauge as a thick wool yarn, you may want to pair them together despite their differences.

Note: At the start of each project, I will recommend yarn based on these categories, which I created to better group my own yarn. To know more about their weight and gauge, refer to the Yarn Chart on page 44.

STEP 3: COLORS

When you have categorized the different types of yarn into yarn categories, you can sort further into different colors or color categories, as stated in the chapter on colors (page 18). If your yarn stash consists of relatively similar colors, you can skip this step.

STEP 4: PROJECTS

Once you've sorted both yarn categories and colors, sort into projects. Is there a yarn category that you have a lot of? Or a color? Perhaps you see some colors in different categories that could go well together?

Use the knowledge you now have about your yarn, and try to place the different skeins into new projects. The projects in this book are based on the Yarn Table and are therefore a good starting point for mapping out further projects. Do you have enough yarn for one or more projects, or do you have to buy some yarn to get enough for an entire project? If you have plans for several projects, you are welcome to divide the various projects into separate project bags or boxes to keep them together.

Yarn Chart

Yarn Weight	Types of Yarns	Gauge Range in Stockinette Stitch	Recommended Needle Range	Categories Used in Projects
Lace	Fingering 10-count crochet thread	33–40 sts	US 000–1 (1.5–2.25mm)	
Super Fine	Sock, Fingering, Baby	27–32 sts	US 1–3 (2.25–3.25mm)	mini wool yarn, thin mohair, thin cotton yarn
Fine	Sport, Baby	23–26 sts	US 3–5 (3.25–3.75mm)	
Light	DK, Light Worsted	21–24 sts	US 5–7 (3.75–4.5mm)	thin wool yarn, cotton yarn
Medium	Worsted, Afghan, Aran	16–20 sts	US 7–9 (4.5–5.5mm)	medium yarn, thick cotton yarn
Bulky	Chunky, Craft, Rug	12–15 sts	US 9–11 (5.5–8mm)	thick wool yarn, blow yarn, thick mohair
Super Bulky	Super Bulky, Roving	7–11 sts	US 11–17 (8–12.75mm)	
Jumbo	Jumbo, Roving	6 sts and fewer	US 17 (12.75mm) and larger	

Abbreviations

st(s): stitch(es)

k: knit

p: purl

inc: increase

dec: decrease

brk (brioche stitch): Where the yarn overs and stitches are knitted together.

Ribbing Stitch Pattern (double purl): 2 x 2 ribbing stitch that is formed from 2 knit stitches and 2 purl stitches.

k2tog: Knit 2 sts together.

ssk (slip slip knit): Pick up 2 sts loosely from the needle one by one as if they were to be knitted. Put the stitches back on the left needle, knit the stitches twisted together.

inc 1 st: Pick up the thread between 2 stitches and make a loop with the thread. Knit the loop right.

m1r (make 1 right): Pick up the thread between 2 stitches and make a loop with the thread. Knit the loop right.

m1l (make 1 left): Pick up the thread between 2 stitches and make a loop with the thread. Knit the loop twisted right.

The Zero-Waste Collection

Share your creations with the knitting community using the hashtags at the start of each project. I'd love to see your unique garment!

Sunset Over the City Sweater

Sunset was the start of my leftover yarn adventure and the first sweater I knitted in the collection. This sweater made me realize how fun the randomness that comes with knitting with leftover yarn can be, and how it's the unpredictability that makes leftover yarn projects truly unique.

The sweater was originally only going to be knitted in pink and purple, but when I started to run out of purple mohair, I realized I had to come up with something. I went back to my yarn stash and found an orange yarn that I added to the project. Then when I started to run out of orange, I found a dark purple thread and added that too. The plan was to knit a plain sweater, but these accidents and my uncertainty made the sweater completely unique. There is no doubt that the color transitions on the sweater have received the most attention and compliments in the end.

SIZES: XS · S · M · L · XL · XXL · 3XL
Circumference: 40" · 42½" · 45" · 49½" · 52" · 54½" · 56¾" (101.6 · 108 · 114.3 · 125.7 · 132.1 · 138.4 · 144.1cm)
Length: 19½" · 20½" · 21¼" · 22" · 22¾" · 23½" · 24½" (49.5 · 52.1 · 54 · 55.8 · 57.8 · 59.7 · 62.2cm)

GAUGE:
9 sts x 14 rounds in stockinette stitch = 4" x 4" (10.2 x 10.2cm)

TOOLS:
US 8 (5mm) circular needle, 16" and 32" (40.6 and 81.3cm) cords
US 10 (6mm) circular needle, 16" and 32" (40.6 and 81.3cm) cords

YARN:
9 · 10.5 · 10.5 · 12.5 · 14 · 15 · 16oz (250 · 300 · 300 · 350 · 400 · 425 · 450g) thick mohair yarn
16 · 16 · 17.5 · 19.5 · 19.5 · 20 · 20oz (450 · 450 · 500 · 550 · 550 · 575 · 575g) blow yarn
4.5 · 5 · 5 · 5 · 5 · 6 · 6oz (125 · 150 · 150 · 150 · 150 · 175 · 175g) mini wool yarn

DECREASES IN BRIOCHE

K2tog: The first st on the left row is a brk. Knit the brk and the next st together, move the st just formed back on the left needle, slip the next brk on the left needle over the st (as if dropping a st), and move the st back on the right needle.

Ssk: The first st on the left row is a brk. Loosely slip off the brk, knit the next 2 sts together and slip the "loose" brk over the newly formed st (as if you are dropping a st).

SAMPLE SWATCH

Cast on 9 sts. Knit stockinette stitch as follows:

Row 1 (wrong side): Knit 1 st (edge stitch). *Knit 1 st, yarn over, and slip the next stitch purl off.* Repeat from * to * until there are 2 sts left on the needle. Knit these two sts.

Row 2 (right side): Knit 1 st (edge stitch). *Yarn over, slip 1 purl st, knit 1 brk.* Repeat from * to * until there are 2 sts left on the needle. Yarn over, slip 1 st purl, knit 1 sl st (edge stitch).

Row 3 (wrong side): Knit 1 st (edge stitch). *Knit 1 brk, yarn over, and slip 1 st purl off.* Repeat from * to * until there are 2 sts left on the needle. Yarn over, and slip 1 st purl, knit 1 brk (edge stitch).

Repeat Rows 2 and 3 a total of 11 times. If the gauge is correct, the swatch should measure 4¾" x 4¾" (12.1 x 12.1cm). Bind off.

BACK PIECE

Cast on 21 · 19 · 21 · 21 · 23 · 21 · 23 sts on US 10 (6mm) circular needle with a strand of blow yarn, a strand of mini wool yarn, and a strand of thick mohair. Work brioche pattern as follows:

Row 1 (wrong side): Knit 1 st (edge stitch). *Knit 1 st, yarn over, and slip the next stitch purl off.* Repeat from * to * until there are 2 sts left on the needle. Knit these two sts.

Row 2 (right side): Knit 1 st (edge stitch). *Yarn over, and slip 1 st purl, knit 1 st (brk).* Repeat from * to * until there are 2 sts left on the needle. Yarn over, and slip 1 st purl, knit 1 sl st (edge stitch).

Row 3 (wrong side): Knit 1 st (edge stitch). *Knit 1 brk, yarn over, and slip 1 st purl. Repeat from * to * until there are 2 sts left on the needle. Yarn over, slip 1 st purl, knit 1 brk (edge stitch).

Furthermore, stockinette stitch must be knitted at the same time as each right side is increased. Knit like this:

Row 1 (right side): Knit 1 st, knit 3 stitches in garter stitch, *knit the next garter st without slipping the st from the needle, yarn over, then knit the stitch one more time = 2 sts increased.* Repeat * to *. Continue the needle in stockinette stitch until there are 5 sts left on the needle and the next st is a stockinette st. Knit 3 sts brk and finish with 1 st.

Row 2 (wrong side): Knit as usual until where you have just increased. *Yarn over, slip 1 st purl off, knit 1 st, yarn over, slip 1 st purl off.* Continue in brk to the next stitch where you have increased. Repeat * to *.

Repeat these two rows a total of 4 · 5 · 5 · 6 · 6 · 7 · 7 times until you have increased 16 · 20 · 20 · 24 · 24 · 28 · 28 sts = 37 · 39 · 41 · 45 · 47 · 49 · 51 sts on the needle. Continue in stockinette stitch until the piece measures 9½" · 9½" · 10¼" · 10¼" · 11" · 11" · 11¾" (24.1 · 24.1 · 26 · 26 · 27.9 · 27.9 · 29.8cm) from the cast-on edge. Make sure the last row is from the wrong side. Cut the thread and let the stitches of the back piece rest on an auxiliary thread or a stitch holder.

LEFT SHOULDER

Pick up 9 · 9 · 9 · 9 · 9 · 9 · 9 sts along the stitches you increased on the left side of the back piece with a strand of blow yarn, a strand of thick mohair, and a strand of mini wool yarn on US 10 (6mm) needle. Knit back and forth in brk as follows:

Row 1 (wrong side): Knit 1 st (edge stitch). *Knit 1 brk, yarn over, and slip the next stitch purl off.* Repeat from * to * until there are 2 sts left on the needle. Knit these two sts.

Row 2 (right side): Knit 1 sl st (edge stitch). *Yarn over, slip 1 st purl, knit 1 brk.* Repeat * to * until 2 sts remain on the needle. Yarn over, slip 1 st purl off, knit 1 brk (edge stitch).

Row 3 (wrong side): Knit 1 st (edge stitch). *Knit 1 brk, yarn over, and slip the next stitch purl off.* Repeat from * to * until there are 2 sts left on the needle. Knit these two sts.

Repeat Row 2 and 3 a total of 6 times for all sizes. You should also knit stockinette stitch while increasing stitches on the right side:

Row 1 (right side): Knit 1 st, knit 3 sts, *knit the next stitch without slipping the sts off the needle, yarn over, then knit the stitch one more time = 2 sts

increased.* Continue in stockinette stitch across the needle and finish with 1 st.

Row 2 (wrong side): Knit as usual until where you have just increased. Yarn over, slip 1 st purl off, knit 1 st, yarn over, slip 1 st purl off. Knit 3 sts and finish with 1 st.

Knit these two needles a total of 2 · 3 · 3 · 4 · 4 · 5 · 5 times = 4 · 6 · 6 · 8 · 8 · 10 · 10 sts increased. You now have 13 · 15 · 15 · 17 · 17 · 19 · 19 sts on the left shoulder. Make sure the last row is from the wrong side. Cut the thread and place stiches on hold on the needle.

RIGHT SHOULDER

Pick up 9 · 9 · 9 · 9 · 9 · 9 · 9 sts along the stitches you increased on the right side of the back piece with a strand of blow yarn, a strand of thick mohair, and a strand of mini wool yarn on US 10 (6mm) needle. Knit back and forth in brk as follows:

Row 1 (wrong side): Knit 1 st (edge stitch). *Knit 1 brk, yarn over, and slip the next stitch purl off.* Repeat from * to * until there are 2 sts left on the needle. Knit these two sts.

Row 2 (right side): Knit 1 st (edge stitch). *Yarn over, and slip 1 purl st, knit 1 brk.* Repeat from * to * until there are 2 sts left on the needle. Throw around the needle and slip 1 st purl, knit 1 brk (edge stitch).

Row 3 (wrong side): Knit 1 st (edge stitch). *Knit 1 brk, yarn over, and slip next stitch purl off.* Repeat from * to * until there are 2 sts left on the needle. Knit these two sts.

Repeat Row 2 and 3 a total of 6 times for all sizes. You should also knit stockinette stitch while increasing stitches on the right side:

Row 1 (right side): Knit 1 st, knit until there are 5 sts left on the needle and the next st is a brk. Knit the next brk without slipping the st from the needle, yarn over, then knit the stitch one more time = 2 sts increased. Knit 3 sts and finish with 1 st.

Row 2 (wrong side): Knit as usual until where you have just increased. Yarn over, slip 1 st purl off, knit 1 st, yarn over, slip 1 st purl off. Work the needle out in garter stitch, and finish with 1 st.

Work these two rows a total of 2 · 3 · 3 · 4 · 4 · 5 · 5 times = 4 · 6 · 6 · 8 · 8 · 10 · 10 sts increased. You now have 13 · 15 · 15 · 17 · 17 · 19 · 19 sts on the right shoulder. Make sure the last row is from the wrong side. Don't cut the thread.

FRONT PIECE

Now the shoulders must be united, and at the same time, stitches for the neck are cast on between the shoulders.

Continue knitting with the yarn end of the right shoulder. Knit over the stitches on the right shoulder without increasing. Then cast on 11 · 9 · 11 · 13 · 11 · 11 · 13 sts with a loop arrangement between the right and left shoulder. Knit over the stitches for the left shoulder in brk, without increasing. You now have 37 · 39 · 41 · 45 · 47 · 49 · 51 sts on the front piece. Knit until the piece measures 11" · 11" · 11¾" · 11¾" · 12½" · 12½" · 13½" (28 · 28 · 30 · 30 · 31.8 · 31.8 · 34.3cm). Make sure that the last row that is knitted is from the wrong side. Don't cut the thread.

TORSO

Continue knitting with the yarn end of the front piece. Knit the stitches of the front piece as before, cast on 1 · 1 · 1 · 1 · 1 · 1 · 1 st with loop casting for armhole. Put the stitches of the back piece onto the needle and knit the stitches of the back piece, cast on 1 · 1 · 1 · 1 · 1 · 1 · 1 st with a loop cast on for the armhole. You now have 76 · 80 · 84 · 92 · 96 · 100 · 104 sts on the needle. Insert a stitch marker. Furthermore, it should be knitted in the round in garter stitch as follows:

Round 1: *Yarn over, slip 1 purl st, knit 1 brk purl.* Repeat * to * until the round.

Round 2: *Knit 1 brk, yarn over, and slip the next stitch purl.* Repeat * to * until the round.

Knit until the piece measures 17½" · 18" · 19" · 19½" · 20½" · 21¼" · 22" (44.4 · 45.7 · 48.3 · 49.5 · 52.1 · 54 · 55.8cm) from the neck, in the middle of the back piece or to the desired length.

Switch to US 8 (5mm) needle and knit 1 round. Work double purl (K2, P2) rib 3" (7.6cm). Bind off with Italian tubular bind off for the prettiest result.

TIP

When you knit the neck and sleeves of the torso, the sweater will contract a little and stay slightly shorter the measurements here. Take into account that the sweater contracts by ¾" (1.9cm). Feel free to knit the sleeves and neck before you start the purl to make sure you get it the length you want.

NECK

Pick up and knit approx. 40 · 40 · 40 · 44 · 44 · 48 · 48 sts with US 8 (5mm) needle around the neck opening. Work double purl (K2, P2) rib until the neck measures 5½" (14cm) or desired length. Bind off with Italian tubular bind off.

SLEEVES

On the sleeves, several things happen at the same time, so it might be a good idea to read the whole section before you start to knit.

Start on the underside of the sleeve and pick up 40 · 40 · 42 · 42 · 44 · 44 · 46 sts on US 10 (6mm) needle with a thread of blow yarn, a thread of thick mohair, and a thread of mini wool thread. Work in garter stitch and knit until the sleeve measures 15" · 15" · 15¾" · 15¾" · 16½" · 16½" · 17½" (38.1 · 38.1 · 40 · 40 · 41.9 · 41.9 · 44.4cm) or desired length.

At the same time, 4 sts should be bind off every 4" (10.2cm) a total of 4 · 4 · 4 · 4 · 4 · 4 · 4 times = 16 sts

(= 24 · 24 · 26 · 26 · 28 · 28 · 30 sts on the sleeve). Work like this:

Ssk, knit stockinette stitch until there are 4 sts left on the round, k2tog, slip over row and slip 1 st loosely.

Knit 1 row while casting off 0 · 0 · 2 · 2 · 0 · 0 · 2 sts evenly spaced.

You now have 24 · 24 · 24 · 24 · 28 · 28 · 28 sts left on the sleeve. Change to US 8 (5mm) needle and work a double purl table (K2, P2) for 3" (7.6cm).

Bind off with Italian tubular bind off for the prettiest result.

Knit a similar sleeve on the other side.

Tie off all loose threads.

The sweater will stretch slightly during use. Please note that it can also expand during washing.

Steam the sweater instead of washing it to smooth stitches and transitions. Dry the sweater flat after washing.

 You can hem the neck in the usual way if you do not want to use Italian tubular bind off, but be aware that it gives a less elastic edge. If it is then separated too tightly, it can be harder to put on the sweater.

RIGHT: This chunky sweater is not only fashionable— it's also super comfy!

Cables and Coffee Sweater

#ZWNo2

In the back of the closet, I had a thick mohair sweater in multicolored stripes. I had knitted it with the best of intentions but never ended up wearing it. I decided to unravel it, and suddenly I was left with loads of small balls of thick mohair in many different colors. It is these skeins that make up the different colors in the sweater you see in the picture. In addition to the colorful skeins, I had several larger skeins with various shades of light pink that I used as the base color.

This turtleneck is a perfect project to use up small scraps of thick mohair. It lends itself well to being knitted with a play of colors, both with and without a base color, so let your scraps decide how the result should be. The structure and the purl stitches bring the colors together in a nice way, giving you a thick and warm sweater that is perfect on cold days.

SIZES: XS · S · M · L · XL · XXL · 3XL
Circumference: 36¼" · 39½" · 42½" · 45½" · 48¾" · 52" · 55" (92 · 100 · 108 · 116 · 124 · 132 · 140cm)
Length: 18" · 18½" · 20" · 21½" · 22⅔" · 24½" · 25½" (45.7 · 47 · 50.8 · 54.6 · 57.8 · 62.2 · 64.8cm)

GAUGE:
16 sts x 22 rounds in garter stitch = 4" (10.2cm)

TOOLS:
US 7 (4.5mm) circular needle, 16" and 32" (40.6 and 81.3cm) cords
US 8 (5mm) circular needle, 16" and 32" (40.6 and 81.3cm) cords

YARN:
Base color: 10.5 · 11.5 · 12.5 · 13.25 · 14 · 15 · 16oz (300 · 325 · 350 · 375 · 400 · 425 · 450g) thick mohair yarn
Accent colors: 10.5 · 11.5 · 12.5 · 13.25 · 14 · 15 · 16oz (300 · 325 · 350 · 375 · 400 · 425 · 450g) thick mohair yarn

SAMPLE SWATCH

Cast on 20 sts with two strands of thick mohair on US 8 (5mm) needle. Work the diagram below. If the gauge is correct, the swatch should be 4¾" x 4¾" (12 x 12cm).

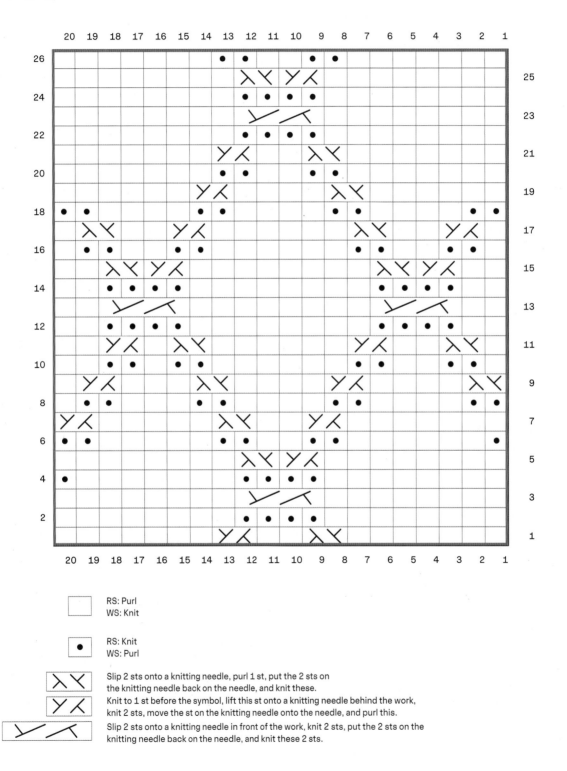

☐		RS: Purl WS: Knit
•		RS: Knit WS: Purl

⅄人	Slip 2 sts onto a knitting needle, purl 1 st, put the 2 sts on the knitting needle back on the needle, and knit these.
⅄人	Knit to 1 st before the symbol, lift this st onto a knitting needle behind the work, knit 2 sts, move the st on the knitting needle onto the needle, and purl this.
⅄人	Slip 2 sts onto a knitting needle in front of the work, knit 2 sts, put the 2 sts on the knitting needle back on the needle, and knit these 2 sts.

DIAGRAM A

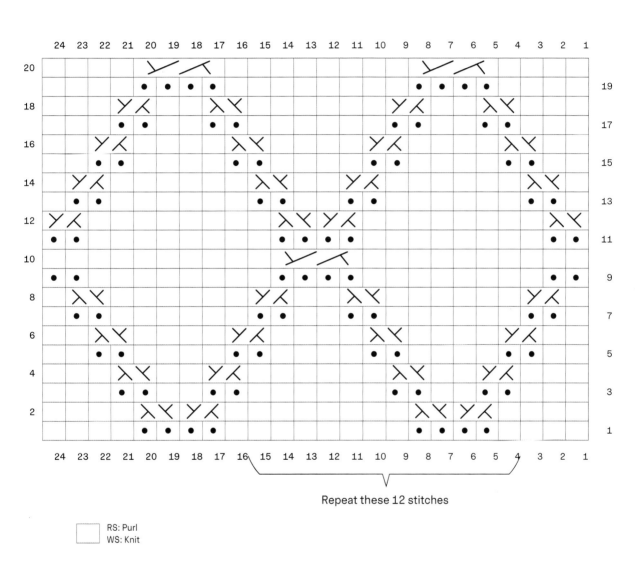

Repeat these 12 stitches

☐	RS: Purl WS: Knit
•	RS: Knit WS: Purl
⋋⋌	Slip 2 sts onto a knitting needle, purl 1 st, put the 2 sts on the knitting needle back on the needle, and knit these.
⋎⋏	Knit to 1 st before the symbol, lift this st onto a knitting needle behind the work, knit 2 sts, move the st on the knitting needle onto the needle, and purl this.
⋎⋏	Slip 2 sts onto a knitting needle in front of the work, knit 2 sts, put the 2 sts on the knitting needle back on the needle, and knit these 2 sts.

RS = Right Side
WS = Wrong Side

TORSO

Cast on 168 · 180 · 192 · 204 · 216 · 228 · 240 sts on US 7 (4.5mm) needle with a double strand of thick mohair. Work (K2, P2) 4" (10.2cm). Switch to US 8 (5mm) needle. Work the cable pattern according to Diagram A until the piece measures 9¾" · 9¾" · 10½" · 11½" · 11¾" · 12½" · 13½" (24.8 · 24.8 · 26.7 · 29.2 · 29.8 · 31.8 · 34.3cm) and the next round is a round where there is no cabling.

Bind off 5 sts at the beginning of the needle. Knit 74 · 80 · 86 · 92 · 98 · 104 · 110 sts as the pattern shows, bind off 10 sts, knit until there are 5 sts left on the needle, bind off the last 5 sts. Let stitches rest on a stitch holder.

SLEEVES

Cast on 48 · 48 · 48 · 56 · 56 · 56 · 56 sts on US 7 (4.5mm) needle with a double strand of thick mohair. Work double purl (K2, P2) rib 4" (10.2cm). Switch to US 8 (5mm) needle and knit 1 round while increasing 0 · 0 · 0 · 4 · 4 · 4 · 4 sts. Work the cable pattern according to Diagram A until the piece measures approx. 9¾" · 9¾" · 6" · 9¾" · 9¾" · 6" · 6" (25 · 25 · 15 · 25 · 25 · 15 · 15cm). Furthermore, a total of 0 · 3 · 4 · 0 · 3 · 4 · 4 times must be increased as follows:

Purl 1 st, inc, purl this stitch. Knit until there is 1 st left on the needle, inc, knit this stitch and the last st in purl = 2 sts increased.

Continue increasing approx. every 4" (10.2cm) = a total of 0 · 6 · 8 · 0 · 6 · 8 · 8 sts increased. The stitches you increase must be purled all the way through and must not be incorporated into the cable pattern.

You now have 48 · 54 · 56 · 60 · 66 · 68 · 68 sts on the needle. Knit until the piece measures approx. 17½" (45.1cm) and the next round is a round where there is no cabling. Bind off 5 sts at the beginning of the round, knit until there are 5 sts left on the round, bind off the last 5 sts = 10 sts.

Knit a corresponding sleeve and place the sleeves on the torso.

CHEST

You now have 224 · 248 · 264 · 284 · 308 · 324 · 336 sts on the yoke.

Knit the first 2 sts on the front piece and insert a stitch marker. Let this be the start of the round. Knit 2 sts, continue working as the pattern shows until there are 4 sts left on the stitches of the front piece. *Knit 2 sts, insert a stitch marker, knit 2 sts.* Work as the pattern shows over the stitches of the sleeve. Repeat * to *. Work as the pattern shows until there are 4 sts left on the stitches of the back piece. Repeat * to *. Work as the pattern shows above the left sleeve stitches.

You now have four stitch markers to mark where it must be joined to raglan. The 2 sts before and after these are raglan stitches and should always be worked in knit.

Knit 1 round as Diagram A shows. The raglan stitches are knitted in the right row. You will then begin to decrease raglan:

Knit 1 st, purl. *Work as the cable pattern shows until 3 sts before your next stitch marker, slip right, knit 2 sts, ssk.* Repeat * to * until there are 3 sts left on the round, k2tog = 8 sts.

Knit 1 round without dec.

Repeat the raglan decreases a total of 19 · 22 · 24 · 26 · 29 · 31 · 32 times = 72 · 72 · 72 · 76 · 76 · 76 · 80 sts left for neck.

NECK

Change to US 7 (4.5mm) needle and knit 6" (15.2cm) K2, P2 rib or desired length. Bind off with Italian tubular bind off.

I love when the weather turns chilly—it's time to break out the sweaters and relax with a nice latte.

Cable-Knit Dickey

#ZWN02

A good and snug dickey is an essential item in any autumn wardrobe and perfect to throw on under a coat, jacket, or large sweater. This project is knitted in thick, fluffy mohair and is well suited for those cold days in autumn and winter. It can be knitted with a base color and an accent color, such as the Cables and Coffee Sweater, or with double thread in the same color as shown here.

SIZES: S · L
Length (measured from the neck down): 10½" · 11" (27 · 28cm)
Width: 11¾" · 12½" (29.8 · 31.8cm)

GAUGE:
16 sts x 22 rounds in garter stitch = 4" (10.2cm)

TOOLS:
US 7 (4.5mm) circular needle,16" and 32" (40.6 and 81.3cm) cords
US 8 (5mm) circular needle, 32" (81.3cm) cords

YARN:
Base color: 3.5 · 4oz (100 · 110g) thick mohair yarn
Accent colors: 3.5 · 4oz (100 · 110g) thick mohair yarn

DIAGRAM A

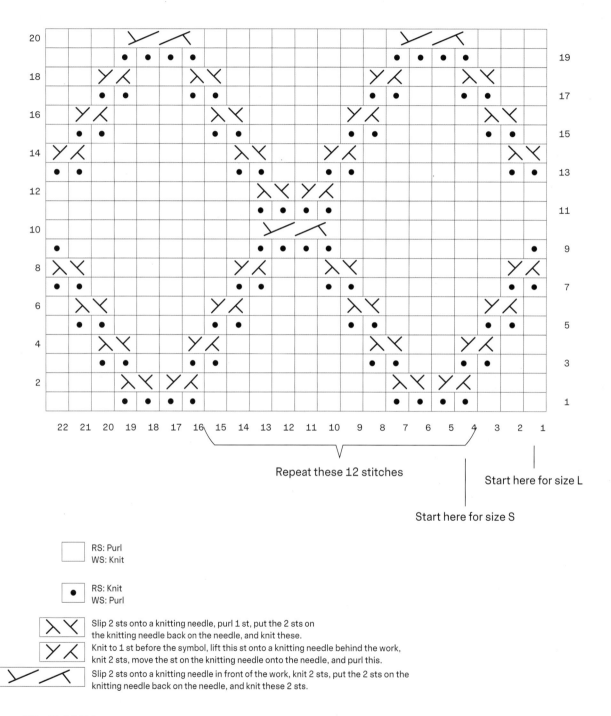

Repeat these 12 stitches

Start here for size L

Start here for size S

RS: Purl
WS: Knit

RS: Knit
WS: Purl

Slip 2 sts onto a knitting needle, purl 1 st, put the 2 sts on
the knitting needle back on the needle, and knit these.

Knit to 1 st before the symbol, lift this st onto a knitting needle behind the work,
knit 2 sts, move the st on the knitting needle onto the needle, and purl this.

Slip 2 sts onto a knitting needle in front of the work, knit 2 sts, put the 2 sts on the
knitting needle back on the needle, and knit these 2 sts.

RS = Right Side

WS = Wrong Side

A dickey is perfect for using up the smallest remnants of thick mohair.

NECK

Cast on 72 · 76 sts with double strand of thick mohair on US 7 (4.5mm) needle. Work 6" (15.2cm) (K2, P2).

Switch to US 8 (5mm) needle, 15¾" (40cm), and knit 1 round in K at the same time as you increase 4 sts evenly distributed = 76 · 80 sts on the needle. Knit 4 sts, insert a stitch marker, increase 1 st, work Diagram A over the next 28 · 30 sts, increase 1 st. Insert a stitch marker, knit 8 sts, insert a stitch marker, increase 1 st. Work Diagram A over the next 28 · 30 sts, increase 1 st, insert a stitch marker, knit 4 sts = 4 sts increased.

You now have 30 · 32 sts on the front piece and the back piece, and 8 · 8 sts on each of the shoulders to the neck = 76 · 80 sts on the needle.

Continue knitting as follows:

Round 1: Knit to your first stitch marker, work as Diagram A shows to the next stitch marker, knit to the next stitch marker, work as Diagram A shows until the last stitch marker, knit in the round.

Round 2: Knit to the first stitch marker, *move the marker to the left needle, increase 1 st, and integrate this stitch into the cable pattern (Diagram A). Work as Diagram A shows until the next stitch marker, increase 1 st, and integrate this stitch into the cable pattern (Diagram A).* Knit to the next stitch marker. Repeat from * to * and knit the rest of the round = 4 sts increased.

Repeat these two rounds a total of 7 · 7 times = 108 · 112 sts.

You now have 46 · 48 sts on the front piece and the back piece, and 8 · 8 sts on each of the shoulders for the neck. Furthermore, you must increase to edge stitches on the front piece and the back piece as follows:

Round 1: Knit to your first stitch marker, work as Diagram A shows to the next stitch marker, knit 8 sts to the next stitch marker, work as Diagram A shows until the last stitch marker, knit 4 sts.

Round 2: Knit to the first stitch marker, move the marker to the left needle, increase 1 st, and knit this stitch. Work as Diagram A shows to the second stitch marker, increase 1 st, and knit this stitch.* Knit to the next stitch marker. Repeat from * to * and knit the rest of the round.

Repeat these two rounds a total of 4 · 4 times, and knit the increased stitches = 124 · 128 sts on the needle. Cut the thread.

Move 31 · 32 sts from the right needle onto the left needle, and insert new yarn so that the round starts in the middle of the back piece. On the next round, bind off the shoulder stitches at the same time that the work is divided into front and back pieces.

Work Diagram A and border stitches until the first stitch marker, bind off 8 sts. Knit until the next stitch marker, bind off 8 sts. Knit to the middle of the back piece where the round started and cut the thread.

You now have 46 · 48 sts on the front piece and the back piece.

Let the back piece's stitches rest on a stitch holder or thread, and start on the front piece.

FRONT PIECE

The first row is from the wrong side. Add yarn and work as follows:

Row 1 (wrong side): Pick up the first purl st off the needle with the thread in front of the piece and knit 3 purl sts. Work as Diagram A shows, purl 3 sts. Knit the last st on right needle.

Row 2 (right side): Slip the first purl st off the needle with the thread in front of the work and knit 3 sts. Work as Diagram A shows. Knit 4 sts.

Repeat these two rows until the piece measures approx. 9½" · 9¾" (24.1 · 24.8cm) from the nape of the neck down.

Knit 6 rows stockinette stitch. Work 2 rows in K1, P1 rib with edge stitches, and bind off with knit stitches.

BACK PIECE

Work like the front piece.

Sew in all threads and steam or wash the dickey before use.

LEFT: This project is perfect for filling out your wardrobe. Make a dickey in every color, and now you're ready to mix and match.

Citrus Sweater-Vest

This vest is knitted with plain yarn as the base color and different colors for the check pattern. To create the squares, you need at least two different colors of thin wool thread. I chose to turn half my thin wool into one continuous color, while the remaining scraps were a mix of different colors.

In this way, I got a continuous orange on the checkerboard pattern, while the rest of the checks changed color. Let the yarn you have determine the colors of the squares—whether it's two or more colors—and see the results.

SIZES: XXS/XS · S/M · L/XL · XXL/3XL
Circumference: 37" · 43¼" · 49½" · 56" (94 · 109.9 · 125.7 · 142.3cm)
Length: 17¾" · 20¾" · 24" · 27¼" (45.1 · 52.7 · 61 · 69.2cm)

GAUGE:
12 sts x 19 rounds = 4" x 4" (10.2 x 10.2cm)

TOOLS:
US 10 (6mm) circular needle, 32" (81.3cm) cords

YARN:
7 · 8 · 9 · 10.5oz (200 · 225 · 250 · 300g) blow yarn
6 · 7 · 8 · 9oz (175 · 200 · 225 · 250g) thin wool thread

SAMPLE SWATCH

Cast on 15 sts with a strand of blow yarn and thin wool thread. Work the check pattern according to Diagram A until you have three squares in height = 3 x 3 checks. If the gauge is correct, the swatch should be 4¾" x 4¾" (12 x 12cm).

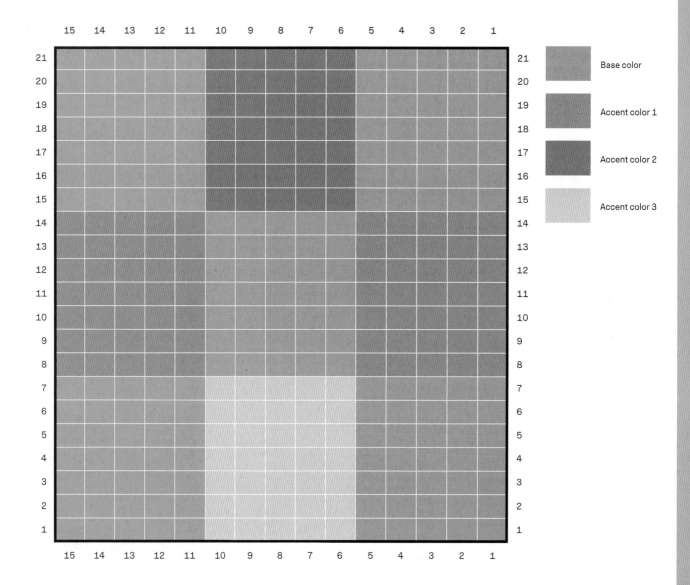

DIAGRAM A: CHECK PATTERN

The vest in the picture is knitted throughout with a thread of blow yarn, while the check pattern is knitted in addition with one thin wool thread.

The squares are knitted with 5 sts x 7 rounds.

When stitches are increased, these must be integrated into the pattern along the way. See an example of how the stitches can be integrated in the diagram on the opposite page.

ABOUT INCREASE

The increases are knitted as follows: Knit until where the increase is to be made, make a loop with the thread between the last stitch you knitted and the next, knit this loop = 1 st increased.

EXAMPLE OF INTEGRATED INCREASE

The lines in the diagram mark where the increases are made. Knit like this:

Row 1: Knit 1 st with base color, increase 1 st with pattern color. Knit out the row as the pattern shows.

Row 2: Purl as shown in the pattern.

Row 3: Knit 1 st with base color, increase 1 st with base color. Knit out the row as the pattern shows.

Row 4: Work as Row 2.

In this way, you integrate the stitches into the check pattern while you knit.

RIGHT SHOULDER BACK PIECE

Cast on 15 · 15 · 20 · 20 sts with a thread of blow yarn and a thread of thin wool thread on US 10 (6mm) needle in a check pattern according to Diagram A from **right to left**. Knit 1 round purl as the pattern shows. Increase like this for all sizes:

Row 1 (right side): Knit 1 st, m1r, integrate the new stitch into the pattern, knit out the row as shown in the pattern.

Row 2: Purl as shown in the pattern.

Row 3: Knit 1 st, m1r, work as the pattern shows.

Row 4: Work as Row 2.

Row 5: Work as Row 3.

Row 6: Work as Row 2 (= 3 increases and you have 18 · 18 · 23 · 23 on the needle).

You have now knitted a total of 7 rows. Cut the thread and let the stitches rest on the needle while you knit the left shoulder.

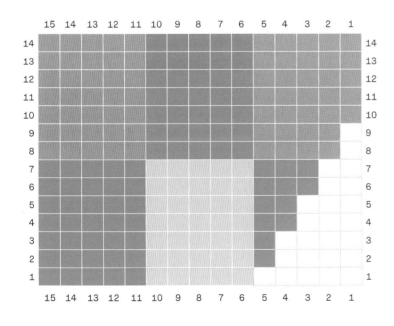

LEFT SHOULDER BACK PIECE

Cast on 15 · 15 · 20 · 20 sts with a thread of blow yarn and a thread of thin wool thread on US 10 (6mm) needle in a check pattern according to Diagram A from **left to right** (start with the opposite color to the color on the right shoulder). Knit 1 P. Increase like this for all sizes:

Row 1 (right side): Work as the pattern shows until there are 1 st left on the needle, inc, integrate the new stitch in the pattern, knit 1 st.

Row 2: Purl as the pattern shows.

Row 3: Knit until 1 st remains on the needle, inc knit 1 st as the pattern shows.

Row 4: Work as Row 2.

Row 5: Work as Row 3.

Row 6: Work as Row 2 (= 3 increases and you have 18 · 18 · 23 · 23 sts on the needle).

You have now knitted 7 rows and will start on the back piece. Don't cut the thread.

BACK PIECE

Knit over the stitches of the left shoulder. Cast on 14 · 24 · 24 · 34 sts with a loop pattern and integrate the stitches into the pattern. Knit over the stitches of the right shoulder. You now have 50 · 60 · 70 · 80 sts on the back piece.

Knit stockinette stitch back and forth as the pattern shows until the piece measures approx. 7¾" · 12¼" · 12¼" · 15⅓" (19.7 · 31.1 · 31.1 · 38.9cm) measured from the shoulder and you have started your 6th · 9th · 9th · 11th square down. Make sure the next row is from the right side. Furthermore, it must be increased to armhole as follows:

Row 1: Knit 1 st, inc. Continue knitting as the pattern shows until 1 st remains on the needle. M1l and knit 1 st.

Row 2: Work (K1, P1) as the pattern shows.

Row 3: Work as the pattern shows.

Row 4: Work as Row 2.

Repeat these 4 rows a total of 3 · 3 · 3 · 3 times. Furthermore, every other round is increased as follows:

Row 1: Knit 1 st, m1r. Work as the pattern shows until you have 1 st left on the needle. Increase purl, knit 1 st.

Row 2: Work (K1, P1) as the pattern shows.

Repeat these rows 2 · 2 · 2 · 2 times. You have now increased 5 · 5 · 5 · 5 sts on each side of the back piece = 60 · 70 · 80 · 90 sts on the back piece.

Cut the thread and place stiches on hold on a stitch holder or thread while the front piece is knitted.

LEFT SHOULDER FRONT PIECE

Pick up 15 · 15 · 20 · 20 sts with a thread of blow yarn and a thread of thin wool thread on US 10 (6mm) needle along the cast-on edge to the left shoulder of the back piece. Pick up stitches and work according to Diagram A from **right to left**.

Knit 3 rows as the pattern shows, where the first and last rows are from the wrong side.

Furthermore, it should be increased to a V-neck as follows:

Row 1: Knit 1 st, m1r, integrate the new stitch into the pattern, knit out the row as the pattern shows.

Row 2: Work (K1, P1) as the pattern shows.

Row 3: Work as the pattern shows.

Row 4: Work as Row 2.

Repeat these 4 rows a total of 8 · 13 · 13 · 18 times. On the next row, increase to armhole at the same time you increase to V-neck:

Row 1: Knit 1 st, m1r. Knit until there is 1 st left on the needle, inc, knit 1 st. Integrate the new stitches into the pattern along the way.

Row 2: Work (K1, P1) as the pattern shows.

Row 3: Work as the pattern shows.

Row 4: Work as Row 2.

Repeat these 4 rows a total of 2 · 2 · 2 · 2 times. You have now formed 2 · 3 · 3 · 4 new squares in the pattern at the V-neck and 2 · 2 · 2 · 2 new stitches in the armhole. Cut the thread and place stiches on hold on the needle or a stitch wire.

RIGHT SHOULDER FRONT PIECE

Pick up 15 · 15 · 20 · 20 sts with a thread of blow yarn and a thread of thin wool thread on US 10 (6mm) needle along the cast-on edge to the right shoulder of the back piece. Work according to Diagram A from **left to right.** For the check pattern to go up when the front pieces meet, make sure here that you knit in the opposite color order on the checks than you did on the left shoulder.

Knit 3 rows as shown in the pattern, where the first and last rows are purl.

Furthermore, it should be increased to a V-neck as follows:

Row 1: Knit until 1 st remains on the needle, inc, integrate the new stitch into the pattern, knit 1 st.

Row 2: Work (K1, P1) as shown in the pattern.

Row 3: Work as the pattern shows.

Row 4: Work as Row 2.

Repeat these 4 rows a total of 8 · 13 · 13 · 18 times. On the next row, increase to armhole at the same time you increase to V-neck:

Row 1: Knit 1 st, inc. Knit until there is 1 st left on the needle, m1r, knit 1 st. Integrate the new stitches into the pattern along the way.

Row 2: Work (K1, P1) as shown in the pattern.

Row 3: Work as the pattern shows.

Row 4: Work as Row 2.

Repeat these 4 rows a total of 2 · 2 · 2 · 2 times. You have now formed 2 · 3 · 3 · 4 new squares in the pattern at the V-neck and 2 · 2 · 2 · 2 new stitches in the armhole. On the next row, the two shoulders must be knitted together for the front piece, and it must then be increased to a sleeve gap.

FRONT PIECE

Now knit in rows over the front piece on the right and left at the same time as it is increased for armholes on both sides of the front piece as follows:

Row 1: Knit 1 st, m1r. Knit over the right front piece as shown in the pattern, continue over the left front piece as shown in the pattern, until 1 st remains on the needle, inc.

Row 2: Work (K1, P1) as shown in the pattern.

Row 3: Work as the pattern shows.

Row 4: Work as Row 2.

Furthermore, you must increase every second row (for example, every row where it is knitted straight):

Row 1: Knit 1 st, m1r. Knit until 1 st remains on the needle, inc.

Row 2: Work (K1, P1) as the pattern shows

Repeat these two rows 2 · 2 · 2 · 2 times. You have now formed a new square on each side of the front piece for the armhole = 60 · 70 · 80 · 90 sts on the front piece.

TORSO

K over the sts of the front piece as shown in the pattern, K over the sts of the back piece as shown in the pattern = 120 · 140 · 160 · 180 sts on the needle. Knit in the round until the piece measures approx. 15⅓" · 18½" · 21½" · 24¾" (38.9 · 47 · 54.6 · 62.9cm) measured from the shoulders or the desired length, the last round should be the last before the color is changed.

Knit 1 round with **double-thread** blow yarn on US 10 (6mm) needle. Continue to knit 2½" (6.4cm) twisted purl (1 twisted K, 1 twisted purl). Bind off.

NECK

Start on the back piece and knit up stitches with double-thread blow yarn on US 10 (6mm) needle. Pick up and knit stitches as follows: 17 · 27 · 27 · 37 sts from the back piece, 5 · 5 · 5 · 5 sts on the left shoulder, 32 · 38 · 38 · 44 sts on left side of the neck, 1 st in the middle (marker stitch), 32 · 38 · 38 · 44 sts on the right side of the neck and 5 · 5 · 5 · 5 sts on the right shoulder = 92 · 114 · 114 · 136 sts in total. Insert a stitch marker at the beginning of the round and one before the marker stitch that marks the middle of the V-neck.

Furthermore, knit twisted purl (1 twisted K, 1 twisted purl) at the same time as it is bind off for a V-neck: Knit twisted purl until 1 st before your marker stitch, slip two sts together from the needle as if you had knit them together. Knit the next st and slip the two sts you slipped off the needle over the stitch you just knitted. This way, you form the V with your middle stitch centered.

Continue to knit decreases for a V-neck every round until the purl measures approx. 1½" (3.8cm) from the neck. Bind off.

EDGING

Pick up and knit 78 · 112 · 112 · 138 sts around one armhole, with double-thread blow yarn on US 10 (6mm) needle. Knit 1¼" (3.2cm) twisted purl. Bind off.

Do the same on the other side.

Tie off all loose threads.

RIGHT: By integrating the base color through the checks, this garment looks cohesive no matter what colors you choose.

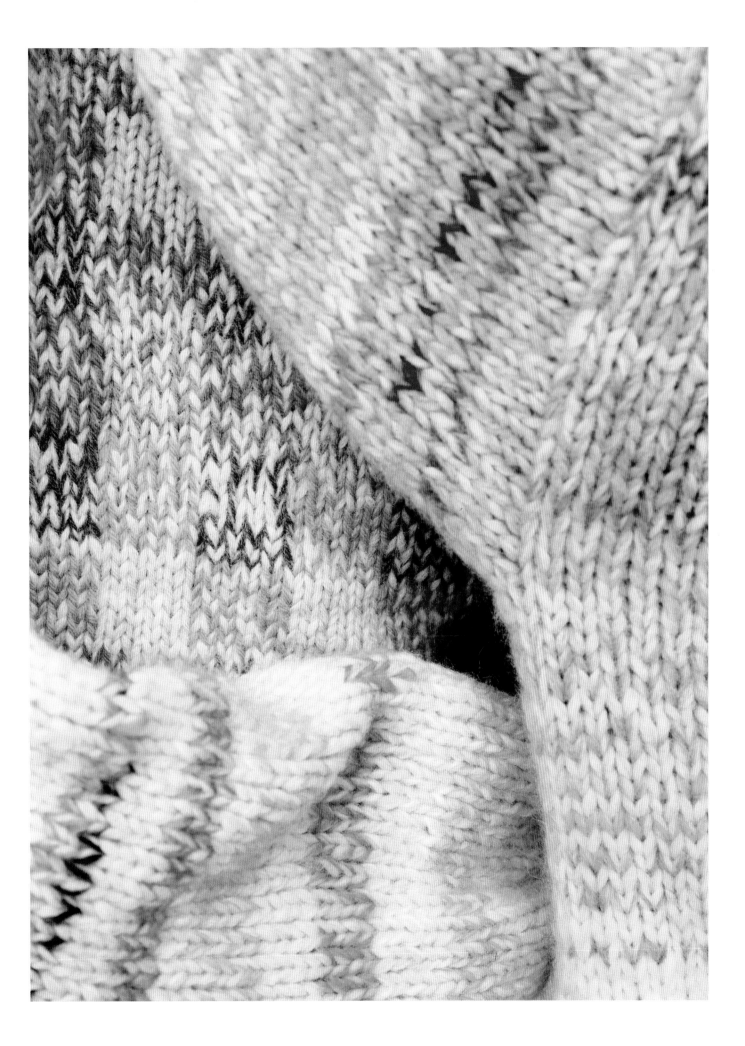

Starry Night Cardigan

#ZWN04

Starry Night is the perfect cardigan to throw over your summer outfit on late summer evenings or to layer in autumn and winter. It is a quick knit with simple techniques that make it a perfect project even for beginners.

The cardigan shown here is knitted with a continuous thread of thick mohair, while the accents made of blow yarn and mini wool thread contains countless different scraps in different colors. The high-contrast base color brings together the diverse color palette in a seamless way, allowing you to experiment a little with colors you initially thought would not go together.

SIZES: XS · S · M · L · XL · XXL · 3XL
Circumference: 37" · 38½" · 41" · 42½" · 44" · 45½" · 47¼" (94 · 97.8 · 104.1 · 108 · 111.8 · 115.6 · 120cm)
Length: 19½" · 20" · 20¾" · 21½" · 22½" · 23¼" · 24" (49.5 · 50.8 · 52.7 · 54.6 · 57.2 · 59.1 · 61cm)

GAUGE:
9 sts x 14 rounds = 4" x 4" (10.2 x 10.2cm)

TOOLS:
US 10 (6mm) circular needle, 16" and 32" (40.6 and 81.3cm) cords
US 8 (5mm) circular needle, 16" and 32" (40.6 and 81.3cm) cords

YARN:
3 · 3.25 · 3.5 · 4 · 4.25 · 4.5 · 5oz (85 · 90 · 100 · 110 · 120 · 130 · 140g) mini wool yarn
6 · 7 · 7 · 8 · 9 · 9.75 · 10.5oz (175 · 200 · 200 · 225 · 250 · 275 · 300g) blow yarn
10.5 · 11.5 · 12.5 · 13.25 · 14 · 15 · 16oz (300 · 325 · 350 · 375 · 400 · 425 · 450g) thick mohair yarn

SAMPLE SWATCH

Cast on 11 sts on US 10 (6mm) needle with a mini wool thread, a thread of thick mohair, and a thread of blow yarn. Knit 17 rows in stockinette stitch. Bind off. If the gauge is correct, the swatch should measure 4¾" x 4¾" (12.1 x 12.1cm).

BACK PIECE

Cast on 28 · 32 · 36 · 38 · 38 · 40 · 40 sts with a mini wool thread, a thread of blow yarn, and a thread of thick mohair thread on US 10 (6mm) needle.

Start by knitting 1 P. Furthermore, increases to the shoulder should be knitted on each side of the back piece like this:

Row 1: Knit 2 sts, m1r knit until 2 sts remain on the needle, m1l, knit 2 sts = 2 sts increased.

Row 2: P.

Repeat these two rows a total of 6 · 6 · 6 · 7 · 9 · 10 · 12 times = 40 · 44 · 48 · 52 · 56 · 60 · 64 sts on the back piece.

Knit until the back piece measures 11¾" · 11¾" · 12½" · 13½" · 14¼" · 15" · 15¾" (29.8 · 29.8 · 31.8 · 34.3 · 36.2 · 38.1 · 40cm) from the neck.

RIGHT SHOULDER

Pick up and knit 12 · 12 · 13 · 14 · 16 · 17 · 19 sts along the stitches you increased at the end of the right side of the back piece. Knit 1 purl, 1 purl, 1 purl. On the next row, start increasing stitches for the neckline. Knit like this:

Row 1: K until there are 2 sts left on the needle, inc, knit 2 sts.

Row 2: P.

Row 3: K.

Row 4: P.

Knit these 4 rows a total of 6 · 7 · 8 · 9 · 9 · 10 · 11 times. You now have 18 · 19 · 21 · 23 · 25 · 27 · 30 sts on the needle.

Knit in stockinette stitch until the piece measures 11¾" · 11¾" · 12½" · 13½" · 14¼" · 15" · 15¾" (29.8 · 29.8 · 31.8 · 34.3 · 36.2 · 38.1 · 40cm) from where you knit up stitches and the next row is from the right side. Cut the thread.

LEFT SHOULDER

Pick up and knit 12 · 12 · 13 · 14 · 16 · 17 · 19 sts along the stitches you increased at the end of the left side of the back piece. Knit 1 purl, 1 purl, 1 purl. On the next row, start increasing stitches for the neckline. Knit like this:

Row 1: Knit 2 sts, m1r, knit row out of needle.

Row 2: P.

Row 3: K.

Row 4: P.

Knit these 4 rows a total of 6 · 7 · 8 · 9 · 9 · 10 · 11 times. You now have 18 · 19 · 21 · 23 · 25 · 27 · 30 sts on the needle.

Knit in stockinette stitch until the piece measures 11¾" · 11¾" · 12½" · 13½" · 14¼" · 15" · 15¾" (29.8 · 29.8 · 31.8 · 34.3 · 36.2 · 38.1 · 40cm) from where you knit up stitches and the next row is from the right side. Don't cut the thread. On the next row, knit together the left shoulder, back piece and right shoulder for the torso.

TORSO

Knit over the stitches of the right shoulder. Cast on 5 · 5 · 5 · 5 · 5 · 5 · 5 sts with a loop cast on, knit over the stitches of the back piece, cast on 5 · 5 · 5 · 5 · 5 · 5 · 5 sts, knit over the stitches of the left shoulder. You have now joined the front pieces and the back piece = 86 · 92 · 100 · 108 · 116 · 124 · 134 sts.

Knit until the torso measures 17¾" · 18" · 19" · 19½" · 20½" · 21¼" · 22" (45.1 · 45.7 · 48.3 · 49.5 · 52.1 · 54 · 55.8cm) measured from the neck. Switch to US 8 (5mm) needle, and work 2" (5.1cm) (K1, P1). Bind off.

SLEEVES

Pick up and knit stitches for sleeves in the stitches along the sleeve gap as follows:

Knit up 2 sts, skip 1 st, repeat from * to * around the entire armhole = approx. 52 · 52 · 56 · 60 · 60 · 64 · 68 sts.

Knit until the sleeve measures 17½" · 17½" · 17¾" · 17¾" · 18" · 18" · 19" (44.4 · 44.4 · 45.1 · 45.1 · 45.7 · 45.7 · 48.3cm) or desired length.

Switch to US 8 (5mm) needle, and knit 1 round while halving the number of stitches as follows:

Knit 2 sts together, repeat from * to * out the row = 26 · 26 · 28 · 30 · 30 · 32 · 34 sts on the needle. Work (K1, P1) for 2" (5.1cm). Bind off.

EDGE

Pick up 1 st for each stitch that is around the entire outer edge of the jacket. If you want to knit the edge without buttonholes, knit 2" (5.1cm) purl and bind off. If you want to knit with buttonholes, follow the step below.

PLACKETS

Knit up stitches and knit ¾" (1.9cm) purl. Measure where you want the buttons on the work so that they are approximately the same distance apart. Place the first buttonhole approx. ¾" (1.9cm) from the bottom edge, and the last buttonhole approx. 4" (10.2cm) from where you last increased to the neck on the shoulder of the front piece. Place a stitch marker on the needle where you want the buttonholes.

Purl until 1 st before your stitch marker, bind off 1 st. Repeat the number of times you have put on stitch markers for buttonholes.

Purl until where you bind off for buttonholes, cast on 1 st. Repeat the number of times you have put on stitch markers for buttonholes.

Knit until the purl measures approx. 2" (5.1cm) and bind off.

Tie off all loose threads.

Bring Back the Eighties V-Neck

#ZWN05

Small checks are the perfect pattern when knitting with leftover yarn, and I decided early on that I wanted to make my very own checkerboard sweater. The result was Bring Back the Eighties.

To create a check pattern, you should have at least two colors, using about half of the total amount of yarn for each color. Please note that if you knit with two colors, the purl should also be knitted in strips so that you use the same amount of yarn in each color here as well. If you want a single-colored purl, you should calculate a little more yarn in this color.

You can also let one half consist of a base color while the other part consists of scraps in different colors. I used a lot of different colors, so it's just a matter of experimenting with what you have! Don't be afraid to run out of a color in the middle of a round—I ran out several times and switched to a color in roughly the same shade without it having any effect on the finished result.

In the project, there is a procedure for striped ribbing. If you want to knit the purl with stripes, you can use this method as a starting point, but feel free to use other colors and create your own twist.

SIZES: XS · S · M · L · XL · XXL · 3XL
Oversize: 37½" · 39½" · 41¼" · 43¼" · 45¼" · 47¼" · 50" (95.3 · 100.3 · 104.8 · 119.9 · 114.9 · 120 · 127cm)
Length: 19" · 19½" · 20½" · 21¼" · 22" · 22¾" · 23½" (48.3 · 49.5 · 52.1 · 54 · 55.8 · 57.8 · 59.7cm)

GAUGE:
18 sts x 18 rounds = 4" (10.2cm)

TOOLS:
US 8 (5mm) circular needle, 16" and 32" (40.6 and 81.3cm) cords

YARN:
10.5 · 11.5 · 12.5 · 13.25 · 14 · 15 · 16oz (300 · 325 · 350 · 375 · 400 · 425 · 450g) thick mohair yarn

SAMPLE SWATCH

Cast on 22 sts on US 8 (5mm) needle with a thick mohair. Work the check pattern as follows:

Round 1: Knit 2 sts with Color 1, knit 2 sts with Color 2.

Round 2: Repeat Round 1.

Round 3: Knit 2 sts with Color 2, knit 2 sts with Color 1.

Round 4: Repeat Round 3.

Repeat these 4 rounds a total of 5 times (20 rounds). Bind off. If the gauge is correct, the swatch should measure 4¾" x 4¾" (12.1 x 12.1cm).

TORSO

Cast on 172 · 180 · 192 · 200 · 208 · 220 · 232 sts with thick mohair on US 8 (5mm) needle. Work (K1, P1) for approx. 1¾" (4.4cm). The purl of the sweater in the picture is knitted in stripes like this:

1 round with dark purple

2 rounds with pink

1 round with blue

3 rounds with yellow

2 rounds of hot pink

Furthermore, stockinette stitch should be worked in a check pattern like this:

Round 1: Knit 2 sts with Color 1, knit 2 sts with Color 2.

Round 2: Repeat Round 1.

Round 3: Knit 2 sts with Color 2, knit 2 sts with Color 1.

Round 4: Repeat Round 3.

Continue working in a check pattern until the torso measures 9¾" · 10½" · 11½" · 12¼" · 13" · 13 ¾" · 36.8" (24.8 · 26.7 · 29.2 · 31.1 · 33 · 34.9 · 36.8cm) and the last round is either Round 2 or 4. On the last round, bind off as follows: Bind off 4 · 4 · 4 · 4 · 4 · 4 · 4 sts, knit 78 · 82 · 88 · 92 · 96 · 102 · 108 sts, bind off 8 · 8 · 8 · 8 · 8 · 8 · 8 sts, knit until 4 · 4 · 4 · 4 · 4 · 4 · 4 sts remain, bind off these 4 · 4 · 4 · 4 · 4 · 4 · 4 sts.

SLEEVES

Cast on 52 · 56 · 56 · 60 · 60 · 64 · 64 sts on US 8 (5mm) needle. Work (K1, P1) in the same color as the body. Work in a check pattern until the sleeve measures approx. 15" · 15¾" · 16½" · 17½" · 18" · 19" · 19" (38.1 · 40 · 41.9 · 44.4 · 45.7 · 48.3 · 48.3cm) or desired length. Bind off 4 · 4 · 4 · 4 · 4 · 4 · 4 sts at the beginning of the round, work as the pattern shows until 4 · 4 · 4 · 4 · 4 · 4 · 4 sts remain on the sleeve, bind off 4 · 4 · 4 · 4 · 4 · 4 · 4 sts.

CHEST

Put the sleeves on the torso. Put on a stitch marker at the beginning and end of each of the sleeves for a total of 4 knitting markers. These mark where you will bind off for the raglan. You should now have 44 · 48 · 48 · 52 · 52 · 56 · 56 sts on each of the sleeves, 78 · 82 · 88 · 92 · 96 · 102 · 108 sts on the front piece and on the back piece = 244 · 260 · 272 · 288 · 296 · 316 · 328 sts on needle.

Start between the left sleeve and the back piece. Knit 4 rounds for all sizes as the pattern shows. On the next round, it will be divided into raglan every second round:

Knit 1 st, purl. Knit until there are 3 sts left before your first stitch marker: *k2tog. Knit 1 st, slip the stitch marker onto the left needle, knit 1 st, purl.* Knit to 3 sts before your next stitch marker, repeat * to *. Knit until 3 sts before your last stitch marker, repeat * to * = 8 sts in total. Knit 1 row as the pattern shows without dec.

Knit until you have dec for raglan a total of 2 · 2 · 2 · 4 · 4 · 5 · 6 times = 228 · 244 · 256 · 256 · 264 · 276 · 280 sts on the needle, and the next round is a round without dec. Cut the thread. It must now be split into a V-neck.

Place the first 37 · 39 · 42 · 42 · 44 · 46 · 48 sts on the left needle over the right needle. Turn the work and purl over all the stitches as shown in the pattern. Furthermore, you must bind off for a V-neck at the same time as you knit castoffs for raglan:

Round 1: Turn the piece again. Knit 2 sts, pull the back st over the front = 1 st space. Bind off to raglan as before and knit to 2 sts before splitting the work into a V-neck. Knit 2 sts together.

Round 2: Turn the piece and knit over all sts as shown in the pattern.

Repeat these two rows a total of 5 · 6 · 6 · 6 · 6 · 7 · 7 times = 178 · 184 · 196 · 196 · 204 · 206 · 210. Furthermore, you must bind off for V-neck and raglan every two rounds as before, but no stitches must be bind off on the front piece. Knit like this: Knit 2 sts, pull the back st over the front = 1 st space. Knit until your first stitch marker, slip the stitch marker onto the right needle, knit 1 st, purl. Knit until 3 sts before your next stitch marker, *k2tog. Knit 1 st, slip the stitch marker onto the left needle, knit 1 st, purl.* Continue to your next stitch marker, repeat * to *. Knit to 3 sts before your last stitch marker, k2tog, work as the pattern shows over the stitches of the front piece without dec to raglan until there are 2 sts left on the needle, knit these 2 sts together. Turn the work over and work as shown in the pattern.

Bind off every other round for a total of 12 · 12 · 12 · 12 · 13 · 13 · 13 times = 82 · 88 · 100 · 100 · 100 · 102 · 106 sts on the needle.

Furthermore, all the stitches except the stitches to shoulder joint of:
Bind off 11 · 12 · 13 · 13 · 11 · 10 · 10 sts. Knit 16 · 16 · 20 · 20 · 24 · 24 · 26 sts = right shoulder stitches. Bind off the stitches of the back piece. Knit 16 · 16 · 20 · 20 · 24 · 24 · 26 sts = left shoulder stitches. Bind off 11 · 12 · 13 · 13 · 11 · 10 · 10 sts.

Furthermore, the stitches of the shoulders must be knitted together like this:
Start with the right shoulder and let the left shoulder's stitches rest on a stitch holder or thread. Place the first 8 · 8 · 10 · 10 · 12 · 12 · 13 stitches on a US 8 (5mm) double-pointed needle or circular needle with a 16" (40.6cm) cord. Place the needles against each other so that the shoulder is folded in the middle and add yarn. *Knit 1 st from each of the needles K together = 2 sts K together. Repeat. Pull the first stitch you knitted together over the second = first stitch.* Repeat * to * over the rest of the stitches on the right shoulder.
Repeat on the left shoulder.

NECK

Knit up 1 st between the right shoulder and the back piece, knit up 32 · 36 · 38 · 38 · 38 · 38 · 40 sts on the back piece, knit up 1 st between the left shoulder and the back piece, knit up 38 · 40 · 42 · 42 · 42 · 42 · 44 sts on the left side of the V-neck, 1 st in the middle (marker), and 38 · 40 · 42 · 42 · 42 · 42 · 44 sts on the right side of the V-neck = 111 · 119 · 125 · 125 · 125 · 131 · 137 sts in total. Put on 1 stitch marker at the beginning of the round and 1 just before the marker stitch in the middle of the V-neck.

Work (K1, P1). At the same time, it must be joined to a V-neck like this:

Knit twisted purl until your marker stitch, slip 2 sts together off the needle as if you had knit them together. Knit the next st and go the two stitches you slipped off the needle over the stitch you just knitted. In this way, you form the V with your middle stitch centered. Continue knitting decreases for the V-neck each round until the purl measures approx. 2" (5.1cm) from the neck. Bind off.

The purl of the sweater in the picture is knitted in stripes like this:

Knit 2 rounds with pink.

Knit 2 rounds with hot pink.

Knit 2 rounds with yellow.

Knit 1 round with blue.

Knit 1 round with pink.

Knit 1 round with dark purple.

Bind off with dark purple.

Sew together under the sleeves and fasten all loose threads.

RIGHT: I arranged my yarn to best differentiate between the colors in each row, but you could also "blend" the colors to achieve an ombre effect.

Pink Lemonade Sweater

#ZWN06

Knitting with completely smooth yarn without combining it with mohair or other fluffy yarn types is a little outside my comfort zone. But I had a lot of skeins of medium wool thread and wanted to challenge myself to knit a garment without hiding the stitch texture. I had a lot of different colors and couldn't use the color-play technique I otherwise swore by.

The idea was to achieve controlled transitions that still made it possible to change color as often as I wanted, so I ended up making a sweater with purple vertical stripes that move with each color change. Horizontally, you can knit as far as you want and change the color whenever you want without disturbing the pattern and the transitions. This sweater is perfect to knit if you have small leftovers of thick threads. I knitted my sweater with purple as the base color of the stripe pattern, but when I saw that I was running out along the way, I decided to knit the purls in pink instead. The base color is intended to extend to both the warp and the stripe pattern.

SIZES: XS · S · M · L · XL · XXL · 3XL
Circumference: 38¼" · 40" · 42" · 44" · 46" · 48" · 50"
    (97.2 · 101.6 · 106.7 · 111.8 · 116.8 · 121.9 · 127cm)
Length: 19" · 19½" · 20½" · 22" · 22¾" · 23½" · 24½"
    (48.3 · 49.5 · 52.1 · 55.8 · 57.8 · 59.7 · 62.2cm)

GAUGE:
21 sts x 20 rounds in pattern knitting = 4" x 4"
    (10.2 x 10.2cm)

TOOLS:
US 8 (5mm) circular needle, 16" and 32"
    (40.6 and 81.3cm) cords

YARN:
Base color: 15 · 16 · 16.75 · 17.5 · 18.5 · 19.5 · 20oz
    (425 · 450 · 475 · 500 · 525 · 550 · 575g) medium
    wool yarn
Pattern color: 12.5 · 13.25 · 14 · 15 · 16 · 16.75 · 17.5oz
    (350 · 375 · 400 · 425 · 450 · 475 · 500g) medium
    wool yarn

PATTERN

The vertical stripes on the sweater are knitted as follows:

Knit 1 st with the base color, knit 1 st with the pattern color. Repeat the round.

Knit this round as long as you want or as far as the yarn will go. Then change the color of the pattern color. Every time you change color, you also change the place of the pattern color and the base color:

Knit 1 st with pattern color, knit 1 st with base color. Repeat the round.

Continue switching between the different colors like this. When increasing and decreasing stitches, these must be incorporated into the pattern. Then there will be a few rounds where there are 2 sts of the same color next to each other, but when all the increases have been completed, the pattern should go up and the stripes should fall on every second stitch.

SAMPLE SWATCH

Cast on 25 sts with a thick woolen thread. Knit vertical stripes in 21 rounds, bind off. If the gauge is correct, the test swatch should measure approx. 4¾" x 4¾" (12.1 x 12.1cm).

LEFT SHOULDER BACK PIECE

Cast on 34 · 35 · 36 · 38 · 39 · 40 · 41 sts on US 8 (5mm) needle. Work 1 row purl with pattern.

Row 1: Knit 1 st, m1r. Include the stitches you increase in the pattern, and knit the rest of the row as follows the star shows.

Row 2: Turn the work over and work over all P.

Knit these two rows a total of 2 · 2 · 3 · 3 · 4 · 4 · 5 times = 36 · 37 · 39 · 41 · 43 · 44 · 46 sts. Cut the thread and place stiches on hold on the needle.

RIGHT SHOULDER BACK PIECE

Cast on 34 · 35 · 36 · 38 · 39 · 40 · 41 sts on US 8 (5mm) needle.

Row 1: K until 1 st remains on the needle, inc. Knit the last st and turn the piece.

Row 2: K over all sts.

Knit these two rows a total of 2 · 2 · 3 · 3 · 4 · 4 · 5 times = 36 · 37 · 39 · 41 · 43 · 44 · 46 sts. Do not cut the thread. You will now knit the shoulders together the back piece.

BACK PIECE

Knit over the stitches of the right shoulder, cast on 29 · 31 · 31 · 33 · 33 · 35 · 37 sts, knit over the stitches of the left shoulder. You now have 101 · 105 · 109 · 115 · 119 · 123 · 129 sts on the back piece.

Knit until the back piece measures 9½" · 10¼" · 11" · 11¾" · 12½" · 13½" · 14¼" (24.1 · 26 · 27.9 · 29.8 · 31.8 · 34.3 · 36.2cm) and the next row is from the right side. Cut the thread and place stiches on hold on a stitch holder or thread.

LEFT SHOULDER FRONT PIECE

Pick up and knit 34 · 35 · 36 · 38 · 39 · 40 · 41 sts with US 8 (5mm) needle from right to left on the left shoulder of the back piece. Knit 1 P. Furthermore, it should be increased to the neckline as follows:

Row 1: Knit 1 st, m1r. Knit the rest of the row.

Row 2: Turn the work over and work over all P.

Knit these rows a total of 4 · 4 · 5 · 5 · 6 · 6 · 7 times = 38 · 39 · 41 · 43 · 45 · 46 · 48 sts on the needle. Cut the thread and place the stitches on a stitch holder or thread.

RIGHT SHOULDER FRONT PIECE

Pick up and knit 34 · 35 · 36 · 38 · 39 · 40 · 41 sts with US 8 (5mm) needle from right to left on the left shoulder of the back piece. Work 1 P. Furthermore, it should be increased to the neck as follows:

Row 1: K until 1 st remains on the needle, inc. Knit the last dc and turn the piece.

Row 2: Work over all sts.

Knit these two rows a total of 4 · 4 · 5 · 5 · 6 · 6 · 7 times = 38 · 39 · 41 · 43 · 45 · 46 · 48 sts on the needle.

FRONT PIECE

Knit over the stitches of the right shoulder.

Cast on 25 · 27 · 27 · 29 · 29 · 31 · 33 sts with a loop arrangement. Then knit straight over the stitches of the left shoulder. You have now 101 · 105 · 109 · 115 · 119 · 123 · 129 sts on the front piece.

Knit until the front piece measures 9½" · 10¼" · 11" · 11¾" · 12½" · 13½" · 14¼" (24.1 · 26 · 27.9 · 29.8 · 31.8 · 34.3 · 36.2cm) and the next row is from the right side. You will now knit together the front piece and the back piece for the torso.

TORSO

Knit over the stitches of the front piece. Cast on 1 · 1 · 2 · 2 · 3 · 4 · 4 sts. Place the stitches from the back piece onto the needle and knit these. Cast on 1 · 1 · 2 · 2 · 3 · 4 · 4 sts. You now have 204 · 212 · 222 · 234 · 244 · 254 · 266 sts on the body.

Knit in stockinette stitch until the torso measures 17¾" · 18½" · 19¼" · 20¾" · 21½" · 22½" · 23¼" (45.1 · 47 · 48.9 · 52.7 · 54.6 · 57.2 · 59.1cm).

Knit 1½" (3.8cm) twisted purl (1 twisted K, 1 twisted P).

Bind off.

SLEEVES

Pick up and knit approx. 94 · 100 · 108 · 116 · 128 · 138 · 144 sts on US 8 (5mm) needle for sleeves.

Knit until the sleeve measures approx. 2" (5.1cm). Furthermore, decrease on the sleeve every 2" (5.1cm) a total of 3 · 3 · 4 · 4 · 5 · 6 · 7 times as follows: Knit 1 st, k2tog, knit until there are 2 sts left on the round, ssk = 2 sts field.

You now have 92 · 94 · 100 · 108 · 118 · 126 · 130 sts on the sleeve. Knit until the sleeve measures 15¾" · 16½" · 17½" · 18" · 19" · 19½" · 20½" (40 · 41.9 · 44.4 · 45.7 · 48.3 · 49.9 · 52.1cm) or desired length. Feel free to try the sweater on and adjust the length accordingly.

Knit 1 round with base color at the same time as dec as follows:

For sizes XS, M, L: Knit 2 sts together, repeat from * to * out the row.

For sizes S, XL, XXL, 3XL: Knit 2 sts together, repeat * to * until 2 sts remain, knit these 2 stitches.

You now have 18" · 19" · 19½" · 21¼" · 23½" · 25¼" · 26" (45.7 · 48.3 · 49.5 · 54 · 59.7 · 64.1 · 66cm). Knit twisted purl (1 twisted K, 1 twisted P), 1½" (3.8cm). Bind off.

NECK

Pick up and knit approx. 74 · 76 · 80 · 82 · 88 · 92 · 98 sts with the base color. Knit twisted (K1, P1) until the neck measures approx. 4¾" (12.1cm). Bind off. Sew or knit the neck down, or leave it as is.

Pin all threads and steam or wash the sweater before use to even out the pattern and transitions.

Golden Hour Cardigan

#ZWN07

This light and airy cardigan is a dream to knit. With thick needles and a cabled pattern, it goes much faster than you might think. Here, I used up quite a lot of leftover thick and thin mohair that I had lying around, and since the cardigan is knitted with two threads, you can easily let the different colors slip into each other by just changing one thread at a time. I chose to keep the colors in the cardigan relatively the same with different shades of yellow and pink, and then I saved the darker shades for the bottom of the cardigan. The cardigan can be knitted in all possible combinations and colors, or plain for a cleaner look.

SIZES: XS · S · M · L · XL · XXL · 3XL
Circumference: 32¼" · 36½" · 41" · 47⅔" · 52" · 54 ½" · 56¾" (81.9 · 92.7 · 104.1 · 121.1 · 132.1 · 138.4 · 144.1cm)
Length: 18" · 19" · 19½" · 20½" · 21¼" · 22" · 22¾" (45.7 · 48.3 · 49.5 · 52.1 · 54 · 55.8 · 57.8cm)

GAUGE:
16 sts x 17 rounds in pattern knitting = 4" x 4" (10.2 x 10.2cm)
11 sts x 15 rounds in stockinette stitch = 4" x 4" (10.2 x 10.2cm)

TOOLS & NOTIONS:
US 8 (5mm) circular needle, 32" (81.3cm) cord
US 8 (5mm) circular needle, 16", 32", and 40" (40.6, 81.3, and 101.6cm) cords
(3) 1" (2.5cm) buttons

YARN:
10.5 · 12.5 · 14 · 16 · 16.75 · 17.5 · 18.5oz (300 · 350 · 400 · 450 · 475 · 500 · 525g) thick mohair yarn
2.75 · 3.5 · 4.5 · 5 · 6 · 7 · 8oz (80 · 100 · 125 · 150 · 175 · 200 · 225g) thin mohair yarn

SAMPLE SWATCH

Cast on 20 sts on US 8 (5mm) needle with one strand of thick mohair and one strand of thin mohair. Work the diagram below. If the gauge is correct, the swatch should be 4¾" x 4¾" (12 x 12cm).

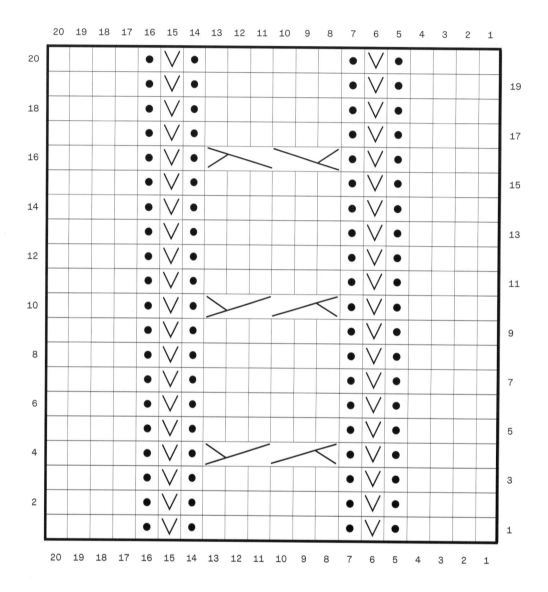

Diagrams found on pages 98–101.

BACK PIECE

Cast on 49 · 49 · 49 · 58 · 58 · 67 · 67 sts on US 8 (5mm) needle with a strand of thick mohair and a strand of thin mohair. Work pattern according to Diagram A while increasing on each side of the piece every other round on the right and left shoulder. The first row is from the wrong side:

Row 1 (wrong side): Work as Diagram A shows.

Row 2 (right side): Knit 2 sts, increase 1 st, work as the diagram shows until there are 2 sts left on the needle, increase 1 st, and knit the last 2 sts. Repeat these two needles a total of 10 · 13 · 19 · 19 · 22 · 22 · 22 times = 69 · 75 · 87 · 96 · 102 · 111 · 111 sts on the needle. Integrate the increased stitches into the pattern as the diagram shows along the way. Work Diagram B until the piece measures 11¾" · 11¾" · 12½" · 12½" · 13½" · 13½" · 13½" (29.8 · 29.8 · 31.8 · 31.8 · 34.3 · 34.3 · 34.3cm) and the next needle is from the right side.

RIGHT SHOULDER

Start at the last stitch you increased to the right shoulder on the back piece, and pick up 20 · 23 · 29 · 32 · 38 · 41 · 41 sts and between the increased stitches and the neck stitches on the back piece. Knit back and forth on the first 7 rows as Diagram C shows, while continuing to cable every 6th round as before. From the 8th row onward, you must also increase every 4th row. The first row is from the wrong side:

Row 1 (wrong side): Work as Diagram C shows from right to left.

Row 2 (right side): Work as Diagram C shows from left to right.

Row 3: Work as Row 1.

Row 4: Work as Row 2.

Row 5: Work as Row 1.

Row 6: Work as Row 2.

Row 7: Work as Row 1.

Row 8: Work as Diagram C shows from left to right until 1 st remains on the needle. Increase 1 st, knit 1 st.

Repeat Rows 5–8 a total of 9 · 9 · 9 · 9 · 9 · 9 · 9 times = 29 · 32 · 38 · 41 · 47 · 50 · 50 sts on the needle. Knit the increased stitches as shown in the diagram. Work until the piece measures approx. 11¾" · 11¾" · 12½" · 12½" · 13½" · 13½" · 14¼" (29.8 · 29.8 · 31.8 · 31.8 · 34.3 · 34.3 · 36.2cm). Finish with a row from the wrong side, and make sure that the last needle is in the same place in the cable pattern as the back piece, so that it is cabled in the same place when the pieces are gathered.

Cut the thread and place stiches on hold on a stitch holder or thread.

LEFT SHOULDER

Start at the neck of the back piece, pick up and knit 20 · 23 · 29 · 32 · 38 · 41 · 41 sts along the stitches you increased to the left shoulder of the back piece. Knit back and forth the first 7 rows as Diagram C shows, while continuing to cable every 6th round as before. Remember that the diagram should be knitted in reverse from how you knitted on the right shoulder. Starting with the 8th row, it must be increased every 4th row while continuing to cable every 6th row as before. The first needle is from the wrong side and is knitted as follows:

Row 1 (wrong side): Work as Diagram C shows from left to right.

Row 2 (right side): Work as Diagram C shows from right to left.

Row 3: Work as Row 1.

Row 4: Work as Row 2.

Row 5: Work as Row 1.

Row 6: Work as Row 2.

Row 7: Work as Row 1.

Row 8: Knit 1 st, increase 1 st, work as the diagram shows from right to left.

Repeat Rows 5–8 a total of 9 · 9 · 9 · 9 · 9 · 9 · 9 times = 29 · 32 · 38 · 41 · 47 · 50 · 50 sts on the needle. Knit the increased stitches as shown in the diagram. Work until the piece measures approx. 11¾" · 11¾" · 12½" · 12½" · 13½" · 13½" · 14¼" (29.8 · 29.8 · 31.8 · 31.8 · 34.3 · 34.3 · 36.2cm). Finish with a row from the wrong side, and make sure that the last needle is in the same place in the cable pattern as the back piece, so that it is cabled in the same place when the pieces are gathered.

On the next needle, gather the shoulders and the back of the torso.

TORSO

Knit over the stitches of the left shoulder, purl the last stitch on the needle. Cast on 1 · 5 · 2 · 8 · 8 · 5 · 10 sts, put the stitches of the back piece onto the needle. Knit the first and last stitch on the back piece purl, and the rest as shown in the pattern. Cast on 1 · 5 · 2 · 8 · 8 · 5 · 10 sts, put the stitches of the right shoulder onto the needle, knit the first st on the right shoulder purl, before knitting the rest of the stitches as the pattern shows.

You have now joined the shoulders and back piece to the torso = 129 · 149 · 167 · 194 · 212 · 221 · 231 and will continue to knit back and forth. Integrate the new stitches so that they fit into the pattern according to Diagram B.

Knit until the torso measures 16½" · 17½" · 18" · 19" · 19½" · 20½" · 21¼" (41.9 · 44.4 · 45.7 · 48.3 · 49.5 · 52.1 · 54cm) or desired length, measured from the neck of the back piece, and the last row is from the wrong side. Change to US 8 (5mm) needle. Knit 1 row. Work (K1, P1) for 2½" (6.4cm). Bind off.

SLEEVES

Pick up and knit 63 · 63 · 72 · 72 · 81 · 81 · 81 sts along the sleeve gap on US 8 (5mm) needle. Work the cable pattern according to Diagram D. Work until the sleeve measures 17¾" (45.1cm) or desired length. Feel free to try the jacket on along the way and adjust the length. Change to US 8 (5mm) needle and knit 1 row at the same time as for size. XS · S shared as follows:

Knit 1 st, knit 2 sts together. Repeat * to * out the row = 21 · 21 · 24 · 24 · 27 · 27 · 27 sts and 42 · 42 · 48 · 48 · 54 · 54 · 54 sts left.

Work (K1, P1) for 2½" (6.4cm). Bind off.

PLACKET

Pick up 1 stitch in each stitch along the edge of the jacket with US 8 (5mm) needle with 40" (101.6cm) cord. Cut the thread and place stiches on hold on the needle. Place 3 stitch markers evenly spaced on the right side of the needle with the stitches you have picked up, marking where the buttonholes should be. Place the first stitch marker on the 8th stitch and the last marker just before the decreases for the V-neck start.

Cast on 14 sts on US 8 (5mm) needle. Furthermore, the placket should be knitted in double knitting at the same time as it is attached to the cardigan by knitting the last stitch on every second needle together with the stitches you knitted up along the edge of the cardigan. Knit like this:

Row 1 (wrong side): Slip the first st off the needle with the thread in front of the work. *Knit 1 st, slip 1 st purl off with the thread in front of the work,* repeat * to * until 1 st remains on the needle, knit this row. Turn the work.

Row 2 (right side): *Slip 1 st purl with the thread in front of the work, knit 1 st,* repeat * to * until 1 st remains on the needle, pick up 1 st from the needle you used to knit up stitches along the edge of the cardigan, and knit this together with the last stitch on the buttonhole.

Repeat Rows 1 and 2 until your first stitch marker. On the next needle, start making buttonholes.

BUTTONHOLES

Row 1: Work 6 sts as Row 2 for placket. Turn the work around.

Row 2: Work 6 sts as Row 1 for placket. Continue back and forth in double knitting over these 6 sts by repeating Rows 1 and 2 (of Buttonhole) a total of 2 or 3 times (**small buttons:** repeat 2 times; **larger buttons:** repeat 3 times). Cut the thread. You will now continue on the next 6 stitches that rest on the placket.

Row 3: Knit 1 st, *slip 1 st purl off with the thread in front of the work, knit 1 st.* Repeat * to * until there is 1 st left on the needle, pick up 1 st from the edge of the cardigan, knit the last st on needle together with the stitch from the edge. Turn the work around.

Row 4: Slip the first st off the needle with the thread in front of the work. *Knit 1 st, slip 1 st purl off with the thread in front of the work.* Repeat * to * over the needle's 8 sts. Turn the piece.

Repeat Rows 3 and 4 a total of 2 or 3 times. Cut the thread. Collect the stitches on a needle and start from the right side.

Repeat Rows 1 and 2 (Placket) until your next stitch marker. Repeat point for buttonhole = 2nd buttonhole.

Repeat Row 1 and Row 2 (Buttonhole) until your last stitch marker. Repeat point for buttonhole = 3rd buttonhole.

You have now finished knitting buttonholes and will continue to knit double knitting around the entire buttonhole post.

Repeat Rows 1 and 2 until you have knitted over all the stitches along the placket. Bind off like this:

Knit 2 sts together twice and pull the back stitch on the needle over the last stitch. Repeat out the row.

Tie off all loose threads. Sew on buttons.

Cabling is a beautiful detail on sweaters, so whether you experiment with color or keep it plain, your garment will look wonderful.

DIAGRAM A

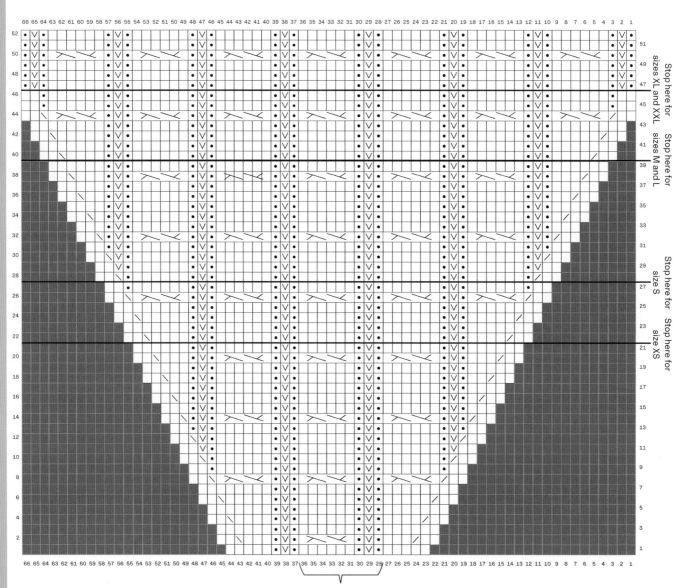

Repeat 4 · 4 · 4 · 5 · 5 · 6 · 6 times

DIAGRAM B

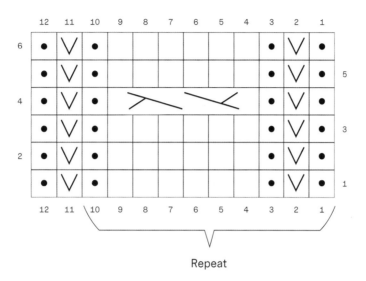

Repeat

DIAGRAM D

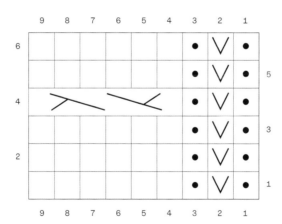

DIAGRAM C

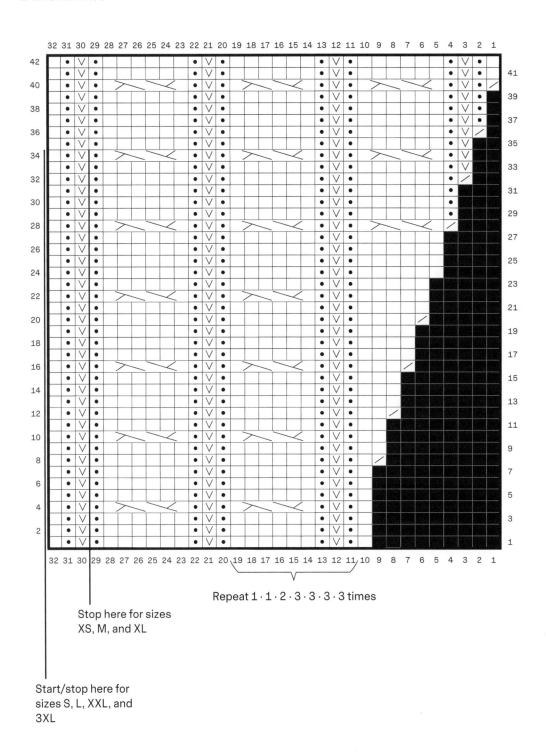

Repeat 1 · 1 · 2 · 3 · 3 · 3 · 3 times

Stop here for sizes
XS, M, and XL

Start/stop here for
sizes S, L, XXL, and
3XL

LEGEND

☐ RS: K
WS: P

⊡ RS: P
WS: K

■ Not knitted

◺ Inc 1 st

Ⅴ RS: K twisted
WS: Knit twisted purl

Slip 3 sts onto a knitting needle and let them rest on the front of the knitting, knit 3 sts, knit the 3 sts on the knitting needle

◹ Increase 1 st

Rainbow Picket Fence Sweater

#ZWNo8

Rainbow Picket Fence is a structured knitted sweater that is knitted from the bottom up, then the sleeves are knitted in and secured with raglan decreases. The sweater is designed to be short, but can be knitted longer if you have enough yarn. The structure is created with something as simple as knit and purl stitches, which creates a nice play in the sweater and makes it easy to change colors without sharp transitions.

If you choose a neutral color as the base color, you can have a color party without it getting too messy. If you have leftovers in neutral colors, you can spice up the sweater by choosing a vibrant color as the base color. Use the smallest scraps you have on the sleeves, and the biggest scraps on the yoke, so you know the scraps will last the whole round. Feel free to try different colors on a sample swatch, which can be used on a later occasion; for example, in the Patchwork Sweater.

SIZES: XS · S · M · L · XL · XXL · 3XL

Circumference: 33½ · 35½ · 37½ · 39½ · 41¼ · 43¼ · 45¼" (85.1 · 90.2 · 95.3 · 100.3 · 104.8 · 109.9 · 114.9cm)

Length: 15¾" · 16½" · 17¾" · 19" · 19½" · 20½" · 21¼" (40 · 41.9 · 45.1 · 48.3 · 49.5 · 52.1 · 54cm)

GAUGE:

19 sts x 29 rounds in structured knitting = 4" x 4" (10.2 x 10.2cm)

TOOLS:

US 4 (3.5mm) circular needle, 16" and 32" (40.6 and 81.3cm) cords

US 6 (4mm) circular needle, 16" and 32" (40.6 and 81.3cm) cords

YARN:

Base color: 9 · 9.75 · 9.75 · 10.5 · 10.5 · 11.5 · 11.5oz (250 · 275 · 275 · 300 · 300 · 325 · 325g) thin wool yarn

Base color: 1.75 · 2.75 · 3.5 · 4.5 · 4.5 · 5 · 5oz (50 · 75 · 100 · 125 · 125 · 150 · 150g) thin mohair yarn

Accent colors: 9.75 · 10.5 · 10.5 · 11.5 · 11.5 · 12.5 · 12.5oz (275 · 300 · 300 · 325 · 325 · 350 · 350g) thin wool yarn

Accent colors: 1.75 · 2.75 · 3.5 · 4.5 · 4.5 · 5 · 5oz (50 · 75 · 100 · 125 · 125 · 150 · 150g) thin mohair yarn

SAMPLE SWATCH

Cast on 25 sts on US 6 (4mm) needle with a thin wool thread and a thin mohair thread in the base color.

Round 1 (wrong side): *Knit 1 st with base color, knit 1 st with pattern color.* Repeat * to * until there is 1 st left on needle, purl with base color.

Round 2 (right side): Work (K1, P1) with pattern color.

Round 3: Work (K1, P1) with pattern color.

Round 4: *Knit 1 st with base color, knit 1 st purl with pattern color.* Repeat * to * out the row.

Round 5: P with base color.

Round 6: *Knit 1 st with base color, purl 1 st with pattern color.* Repeat * to * until 1 st remains on the needle, knit with the base color.

Round 7: Knit with pattern color.

Round 8: Knit with pattern color.

Round 9: *Knit 1 st with base color, knit 1 st with pattern color.* Repeat * to * out the row.

Round 10: Knit with base color.

Repeat these 10 rounds 3 times. Repeat Rounds 1–5 one more time, bind off. If the gauge is correct, you should now have a piece measuring 4¾" x 4¾" (12.1 x 12.1cm).

TORSO

Cast on 172 · 180 · 188 · 200 · 208 · 216 · 224 sts on US 4 (3.5mm) needle, 32" (81.3cm) cord, with a thin wool thread in the base color and a thin mohair thread in the base color. Work around in (K1, P1) until the purl measures 2¾" (7cm).

Switch to US 6 (4mm) needle and knit 1 round. Place a stitch marker at the beginning of the work and after 86 · 90 · 94 · 100 · 104 · 108 · 112 sts (halfway through the work).

Furthermore, you should knit structured knitting as follows:

Round 1: *Knit 1 st with base color, purl 1 st with pattern color.* Repeat * to * out the row.

Round 2: Work (K1, P1) with pattern color.

Round 3: Knit with pattern color.

Round 4: Repeat Round 1.

Round 5: Knit with base color.

Repeat these 5 rounds until the piece measures 9¾" · 10½" · 11½" · 12¼" · 13" · 13¾" · 14½" (24.8 · 26.7 · 29.2 · 31.1 · 33 · 34.9 · 36.8cm) or the desired length. Here, you may want to knit the sleeves and see how much yarn you have left. If you have more than what is stated in the pattern, you can knit the torso a little longer; if you have less, you can knit shorter. The next round to be knitted is a round where the base color is knitted straight. For the stripe pattern in the picture, the color of the pattern color is changed after every 5 rounds.

Bind off 7 sts at the beginning of the round, insert a stitch marker. Knit to 7 sts before your second stitch marker, keep the marker, and bind off 10 sts. Let the work rest until the first sleeve is knitted, so that you can put the sleeve on the support piece before you continue knitting.

SLEEVES

Cast on 60 · 62 · 64 · 66 · 68 · 70 · 72 sts on US 4 (3.5mm) needle with the base color.

Knit 1½" (3.8cm) purl, change to US 4 (3.5mm) needle, and knit 1 round.

Knit structured knitting as on the torso (Rounds 1–5) until the piece measures 7¾" (19.7cm). Furthermore, increases must be knitted on the rounds where you knit with the pattern color. Be sure to integrate the stitches that are increased into the established structure so that the knit and purl stitches in the pattern are not shifted.

Knit 1 sl st, m1l, 1 st, knit until 1 st remains on the sleeve, m1r, knit the last stitch. Repeat * to * approx. every 1½" (3.8cm) a total of 4 · 4 · 5 · 5 · 6 · 7 · 8 times (= 68 · 70 · 74 · 76 · 80 · 84 · 88 sts on the sleeve).

Continue knitting in established structured knitting until the sleeve measures approx. 15¾" · 16½" · 17½" · 18" · 19" · 19½" · 20½" (40 · 41.9 · 44.4 · 45.7 · 48.3 · 49.5 · 52.1cm), and the next round is a round in which the base color is knitted straight. Decrease for armholes on the next round as follows:

Bind off 5 sts at the beginning of the round, knit until 5 sts remain, bind off these 5 sts = 10 sts.

Cut the thread and put the sleeve over the support piece.

Insert a stitch marker in the transition to the body. Continue knitting on the yoke until there are 3 sts left on the round, insert a stitch marker. Bind off these 3 sts and cut the thread.

Let the work rest while you knit another matching sleeve. Put the other sleeve on the support piece.

CHEST

You now have 72 · 76 · 80 · 86 · 90 · 94 · 98 sts on the front piece, stitch marker, 58 · 60 · 64 · 66 · 70 · 74 · 78 sts on the right sleeve, stitch marker, 80 · 84 · 88 · 94 · 98 · 102 · 106 sts on the back piece, stitch marker, 58 · 60 · 64 · 66 · 70 · 74 · 78 sts on the left sleeve = 268 · 280 · 296 · 312 · 328 · 344 · 360 sts on the body piece

Chest is knitted in an established structured knit at the same time as it is bind off to raglan on every round it is knitted straight. Make sure that on rounds where you knit every other base color and purl pattern color, the knit stitches, and purl stitches must always fall in the same place. Therefore, it will vary which mesh the round starts with as it decreases. Knit like this:

Round 1: *Knit 1 st with pattern color, knit 1 st with base color.* Repeat * to * out the row.

Round 2: Work (K1, P1) with pattern color.

Round 3 (pattern color): Ssk, *knit K until 2 sts before your next stitch marker, ssk, move the stitch marker onto the right needle, ssk.* Repeat * to * until there are 2 sts left on the round, k2tog = 8 sts.

Round 4: *Knit 1 st with base color, knit 1 st purl with pattern color.* Repeat * to * out the row.

Round 5 (base color): Ssk, *knit K until 2 sts before your next stitch marker, k2tog, move the stitch marker onto the right needle, ssk.* Repeat from * to * until there are 2 sts left on the round, k2tog = 8 sts.

Repeat these 5 rounds until you have knitted a total of 21 · 22 · 24 · 26 · 28 · 30 · 32 rounds with decreases and there are 100 · 104 · 104 · 104 · 104 · 104 · 104 sts left on the needle. Continue knitting on the pattern without dec so that the last round you knit before you start on the neck is a round where you knit the base color straight.

NECK

Switch to US 4 (3.5mm) needle. Work (K1, P1) until the neck measures 1½" (3.8cm) or desired length. Bind off with the desired bind off.

ASSEMBLY

Sew together under the sleeves. Tie off all loose threads.

Wash the sweater and adjust the shape you want before use. The sweater will expand slightly during washing.

RIGHT: For the color palette on this sweater, I chose mostly pastels. This way, the darker and more saturated colors stand out among the many stripes.

Picket Fence Headband

This headband is perfect if you have leftovers after the matching sweater, or if you want to use up the smallest scraps in your stash. The headband consists of four strips of structured knit, which can be knitted in different colors or in the same color. If you want to knit with different colors, divide the amount of yarn for the pattern color by four to find out how much you need per strip.

The headband is knitted double by knitting the first half of the inside in the base color first, then the front of the headband is knitted with structured knit, and the last part is knitted in the base color. The top and bottom of the work are knitted or sewn together—and you have a double-knitted headband that warms your ears when the cold comes!

SIZES: S · M · L
Circumference: 21¼"–22" · 22½"–23¼" · 23½"–24¾" (54–55.8 · 57.2–59.1 · 59.7–62.9cm)
Width: 3" (7.6cm)

GAUGE:
19 sts x 29 rounds in structured knitting = 4" x 4" (10.2 x 10.2cm)

TOOLS:
US 6 (4mm) circular needle, 16" (40.6cm) cord

YARN:
Base color: 1.25 · 1.4 · 1.6oz (35 · 40 · 45g) thin wool yarn
Base color: 0.4 · 0.5 · 0.5oz (10 · 15 · 15g) thin mohair yarn
Accent colors: 0.6 · 0.7 · 0.8oz (16 · 20 · 24g) thin wool yarn
Accent colors: 0.3 · 0.4 · 0.4oz (8 · 10 · 12g) thin mohair yarn

Cast on 96 · 104 · 112 sts on US 6 (4mm) needle with a thin wool thread in the base color and a thread of thin mohair in the base color. Knit 1½" (3.8cm) in stockinette stitch.

On the next round, knit the edge of the headband:

Round 1: *Knit 2 sts together, yarn over.* Repeat * to * out the row.

Round 2: Knit 1 sl st, knit the yarn over twisted knit.

Repeat Rounds 1 and 2 a total of 2 times.

Furthermore, you must establish structural knitting as follows:

Round 1: *Knit 1 st with base color, purl 1 st with pattern color.* Repeat * to * out the row.

Round 2: Work (K1, P1) with pattern color.

Round 3: Knit rows with pattern color.

Round 4: Repeat Round 1.

Round 5: Knit with base color.

Repeat these 5 rounds a total of 4 times = 4 stripes with structured knitting in pattern color.

Knit edge in the same way as at the bottom of the headband:

Round 1: *Knit 2 sts together, yarn over,* repeat from * to * out the row.

Round 2: Knit 1 sl st, knit the yarn over twisted knit.

Repeat Rounds 1 and 2 a total of 2 times.

Work stockinette stitch 1½" (3.8cm).

Turn the headband over, and fold the cast-on edge and the stitches you have on the needle toward the center of the headband. You will now bind off the stitches on the needle at the same time as you knit them together with the cast-on edge:

Knit 1 st from the cast-on edge together with 1 st from the needle. Repeat * to * and pull the back stitch over the front. Continue like this until all the stitches have been bind off and the cast-on edge is knitted together with the cast-off edge.

Alternative assembly: Bind off with straight stitches. Sew the set-up edge together with the drop-off edge.

Fasten all threads. Steam or block the headband before use.

RIGHT: The Starry Night Cardigan was made in blue and orange, showing just how different an result your color choices can make!

Sorbet Date Halter Top

#ZWN09

Sorbet Date is a ribbed summer top with two long straps that can be tied at the neck and adjusted as you wish. The halter top can be knitted with stripes as indicated in the pattern, but it can also be knitted in a solid color or with thicker/thinner stripes than specified. Let the yarn you have determine how thick you want in each color; you could have thicker stripes in the color you have most of, or let the pattern color stripes consist of small yarn scraps in different colors.

SIZES: XS · S · M · L · XL · XXL · 3XL

Circumference (at waist): 32" · 33¾" · 35¾" · 37¾" · 39¾" · 41¾" · 44" (81.3 · 85.7 · 90.8 · 95.9 · 101 · 106 · 111.8cm)

GAUGE:

21 sts x 30 rounds in stockinette stitch = 4" x 4" (10.2 x 10.2cm)

TOOLS:

US 4 (3.5mm) circular needle, 24" and 32" (61 and 81.3cm) cords

YARN:

5 · 6 · 6 · 7 · 7 · 8 · 8oz (150 · 175 · 175 · 200 · 200 · 225 · 225g) cotton yarn

Stripes (base color): 2.5 · 3 · 3 · 3.5 · 3.5 · 4 · 4oz (75 · 90 · 90 · 100 · 100 · 115 · 115g) cotton yarn

Stripes (accent colors): 2.5 · 3 · 3 · 3.5 · 3.5 · 4 · 4oz (75 · 90 · 90 · 100 · 100 · 115 · 115g) cotton yarn

---

SAMPLE SWATCH

Cast on 26 sts. Knit stockinette stitch back and forth for a total of 36 rows. If the gauge is correct, the swatch should measure approx. 4¾" x 4¾" (12.1 x 12.1cm).

TORSO

Cast on 156 · 164 · 172 · 184 · 192 · 200 · 208 sts on US 4 (3.5mm) needle with a cotton thread in the base color. Knit two rounds of double knit like this:

Round 1: *Knit 1 st, slip off 1 st purl with the thread in front of the work,* repeat from * to * to the end of the round.

Round 2: *Slip off 1 st purl with the thread behind the work, knit 1 st purl,* repeat from * to * to the end of the round.

Change to pattern color and knit 2 rounds in ribbing (K2, P2). Change to the base color and knit 2 more rounds in ribbing. Continue to work ribbing in stripes (2 rounds of pattern color, 2 rounds of base color) until the piece measures 7½" · 7½" · 7¾" · 8¼" · 8⅔" · 9" · 9½" (19.1 · 19.1 · 19.7 · 21 · 22 · 22.9 · 24.1cm) or the desired length and the next round is a round where it is changed to the base color.

On the next round, work double knitting over the stitches of the back before the stitches are bind off. Furthermore, the front piece must be knitted back and forth on its own. If you knit in stripes, the next 5 rounds should be knitted with the base color as follows:

Round 1: Work ribbing over the first 82 · 86 · 90 · 96 · 100 · 104 · 108 sts on the needle. *Knit 1 st, slip 1 st purl off with the thread in front of work,* repeat * to * over the next 70 · 74 · 78 · 84 · 88 · 92 · 96 sts. Knit the last 4 stitches of the round in ribbing.

Round 2: Work ribbing over the first 82 · 86 · 90 · 96 · 100 · 104 · 108 sts on the next round. *Slip 1 purl st with the thread behind the work, purl 1 st,* repeat * to * over the next 70 · 74 · 78 · 84 · 88 · 92 · 96. Knit the last 4 sts on the round in ribbing.

On the next round, the stitches you just knitted in double knitting should be bind off:

Round 3: Knit the first 82 · 86 · 90 · 96 · 100 · 104 · 108 sts of the round as shown in the ribbing pattern. Bind off the next 70 · 74 · 78 · 84 · 88 · 92 · 96 sts as follows: *Knit 2 sts together, knit the next 2 sts together, pull the back stitch over the front stitch = 3 sts bind off in total. Continue to cast like this until there are 5 sts left on the needle, knit 1 st, pull the back st over the front stitch = 4 sts left on the needle. Knit the last 4 sts of the round as the ribbing pattern shows, cut the thread. Slip the last 4 stitches onto the left needle.

FRONT PIECE

You now have 86 · 90 · 94 · 100 · 104 · 108 · 112 sts on the front piece. Knit the first two rows without dec:

Row 1 (right side): Continue with base color. Slip 1 st purl off the needle with the thread in front of the piece. Knit 2 sts. Knit like the ribbing pattern until there are 3 sts left on the needle, knit these. Turn the piece.

Row 2 (wrong side): Slip 1 st purl from the needle with the thread in front of the work, knit 2 sts purl. Continue knitting in ribbing up to 3 sts before the end of the needle. Knit 2 sts purl and 1 st. Furthermore, stripes are to be knitted as before (2 rounds of pattern color, 2 rounds of base color) at the same time as you bind off for armholes on both sides of the front piece each right side a total of 2 times.

Row 3: Change to pattern color. Slip the first st from the needle with the thread in front of the piece, work 1 st, purl, knit until there are 4 sts left on the needle, purl, knit 2 sts. Turn the work.

Row 4: Slip the first st off the needle with the thread in front of the work, purl 2 sts. Continue to knit in ribbing until there are 3 sts left on the needle. Knit 2 sts, K 1.

Repeat these two rows (Rows 3 and 4) a total of 2 · 2 · 2 · 2 · 2 · 2 · 2 times = 82 · 86 · 90 · 96 · 100 · 104 · 108 sts left on the front piece.

Furthermore, the armholes must be bind off on every other right side as follows:

Row 5: Slip the first st of the needle with the thread in front of the work, knit 1 st, ssk, knit until there are 4 sts left on the needle, k2tog, knit 2 sts.

Row 6: Slip the first st off the needle with the thread in front of the work, knit ribbing until there are 3 sts left on the needle, purl 2, knit 1.

Row 7: Slip the first st off the needle with the thread in front of the work, knit 2 rows, continue in ribbing over the rest of the stitches until there are 3 sts left, knit these 3 rows.

Row 8: Knit like Row 6.

Repeat Rows 5–8 a total of 2 · 2 · 2 · 2 · 2 · 2 · 2 times = 78 · 82 · 86 · 92 · 96 · 100 · 104 sts left on the needle. On the next row, the front piece is divided into two sections, which are knitted separately.

LEFT SECTION

Row 1: Slip the first st of the needle with the thread in front of the work, knit 1 st, ssk, knit 31 · 33 · 34 · 38 · 40 · 42 · 44 sts as shown in the ribbing pattern, k2tog, knit 2 sts.

Row 2: Slip the first st off the needle with the thread in front of the work, purl 2, knit ribbing pattern until there are 3 sts left on the needle, purl 2, knit 1.

Place the last 39 · 41 · 42 · 46 · 48 · 50 · 52 sts on the right side of the front piece onto a knitting needle or thread. Furthermore, the neck and armholes must be bind off on both sides of the left part a further 2 times:

Row 3: Slip the first st off the needle with the thread in front of the work, work 2 sts, continue in ribbing over the rest of the stitches until there are 3 sts left, knit these 3 sts.

Row 4: Work as Row 2.

Row 5: Slip the first st of the needle with the thread in front of the work, knit 1 st, ssk, knit until there are 4 sts left on the needle, k2tog, knit 2 sts.

Row 6: Work as Row 2.

Repeat Rows 3–6 a total of 2 · 2 · 2 · 2 · 2 · 2 · 2 times. You now have 33 · 35 · 38 · 40 · 42 · 44 · 46 sts on the needle.

In the next round, only knit to the neck:

Row 7: Slip the first st off the needle with the thread in front of the work, knit 2 sts, knit until there are 4 sts left on the needle, bind off, knit 2 sts.

Row 8: Work as Row 2.

Row 9: Work as Row 3.

Row 10: Work as Row 2.

Repeat Rows 7–10 a total of 1 · 3 · 2 · 4 · 2 · 4 · 6 times = 32 · 32 · 36 · 36 · 40 · 40 · 40 sts on the needle. Furthermore, you must continue to decrease to the neck at the same time as you decrease along the shoulder on the left part:

Row 11: Slip the first st P from the needle with the thread in front of the work. Knit 2 sts, 2 sts purl, 1 st purl. Knit as the ribbing pattern shows until there are 4 sts left on the needle, k2tog, knit 2 sts.

Row 12: Work as Row 2.

Row 13: Work as Row 3.

Row 14: Work as Row 2.

Repeat Rows 11–14 a total of 4 · 4 · 4 · 4 · 4 · 4 · 4 times = 24 · 24 · 28 · 28 · 32 · 32 · 32 sts.

From now on, you will no longer decrease to your neck. Knit like this:

Row 15: Slip the first st P from the needle with the thread in front of the work. Knit 2 sts, 2 sts purl, 1 st purl. Work as the ribbing pattern shows until there are 3 sts left on the needle, knit 3 sts.

Row 16: Work as Row 2.

Repeat Rows 15 and 16 a total of 12 · 12 · 16 · 16 · 20 · 20 · 20 times = 12 · 12 · 12 · 12 · 12 · 12 · 12 sts on the needle.

LEFT STRAP

The strap is knitted the same for all sizes.

Pick up 1 st purl with the thread in front of the work. Work as the ribbing pattern shows until 1 st remains, knit 1 st.

Knit ribbing in base color by repeating * to * until the strap measures 22¾" (57.8cm).

Bind off like this:

Row 1: Slip 1 st purl off the needle with the thread in front of your work, knit 1 st, pull the stitch you slipped over the stitch you knitted row = 1 st space. Work as the ribbing pattern shows the needle and knit the last st.

Row 2: Pick up 1 st purl with the thread in front of the work, work as the ribbing pattern shows until there is 1 st left on the needle, knit this st. Pull the last stitch on the needle over the penultimate stitch = 1 stitch. Turn the work around.

Repeat these 2 rows a total of 11 times until 1 st remains on the needle. Pull your thread through this stitch. You will now start on the right section of the front piece.

RIGHT SECTION

Add yarn and start on the right side of the right section.

Row 1 (right side): Slip the first st of the needle with the thread in front of the work, knit 1 st, ssk, knit 31 · 33 · 34 · 38 · 40 · 42 · 44 sts as shown in the ribbing pattern, k2tog, knit 2 sts.

Row 2 (wrong side): Slip the first st of the needle with the thread in front of the work, purl 2 sts, knit ribbing until there are 3 sts left on the needle, purl 2 sts, knit 1.

Furthermore, the neck and armholes must be bind off on both sides of the left part a further 2 times:

Row 3: Slip the first st off the needle with the thread in front of the work, knit 2 rows, continue in ribbing over the rest of the stitches until there are 3 sts left, knit these 3 rows.

Row 4: Work as Row 2.

Row 5: Slip the first st of the needle with the thread in front of the work, knit 1 st, ssk, knit until there are 4 sts left on the needle, k2tog, knit 2 sts.

Row 6: Work as Row 2.

Repeat Rows 3–6 a total of 2 · 2 · 2 · 2 · 2 · 2 · 2 times. You now have 33 · 35 · 38 · 40 · 42 · 44 · 46 sts on the needle.

In the next round, only knit to the neck:

Row 7: Slip the first st off the needle with the thread in front of the work, knit 1 st, purl, knit ribbing pattern until there are 3 sts left on the needle, knit these 3 sts = 32 sts on the needle.

Row 8: Work as Row 2.

Row 9: Work as Row 3.

Row 10: Work as Row 2.

Repeat Rows 7–10 in total 1 · 3 · 2 · 4 · 2 · 4 · 6 times = 32 · 32 · 36 · 36 · 40 · 40 · 40 sts on the needle.

Furthermore, you must continue to decrease to the neck at the same time as you decrease along the shoulder on the right side:

Row 11: Slip the first st purl off the needle with the thread in front of the work, knit 1 st, ssk, work the ribbing pattern shows until there are 8 sts left on the needle, k2tog. Knit 1 st, 2 sts purl, and finish with 3 sts.

Row 12: Work as Row 2.

Row 13: Work as Row 3.

Row 14: Work as Row 2.

Repeat Rows 11–14 a total of 4 · 4 · 4 · 4 · 4 · 4 · 4 times = 24 · 24 · 28 · 28 · 32 · 32 · 32 sts on the needle. From now on, you will no longer decrease to your neck. Knit like this:

Row 15: Slip the first purl st from the needle with the thread in front of the work, knit 2 sts, work as the ribbing pattern shows until there are 8 sts left on the needle, k2tog. Knit 1 st, 2 sts purl, and finish with 3 sts.

Row 16: Work as Row 2.

Repeat Rows 15–16 a total of 12 · 12 · 16 · 16 · 20 · 20 · 20 times = 12 · 12 · 12 · 12 · 12 · 12 · 12 sts on the needle.

RIGHT STRAP

Knit like the left strap.

Fasten all loose threads and wash the top before use.

RIGHT: Make the straps on this halter top as long or short as you like. You could even add stripes or other details to make it your own.

Patchwork Cardigan

#ZWNo10

Do you think it's boring to knit swatches like I do? When I started my scrap yarn project, I had this cardigan in mind almost from the beginning. It made the test-swatch knitting a little more fun and motivating.

When knitting with leftover yarn, knitting a gauge is perhaps the most important step you do—not only to check the tension, but also to test out different color combinations. This jacket has become a favorite and is perhaps the coolest garment I have ever made. And since you need minimal yarn per swatch, and can knit with countless combinations of yarn, this is perhaps the ultimate leftover yarn project because it is suitable for using up even the smallest leftovers.

SIZES: S · L

Width (measured flat): 15" · 24½" (38.1 · 62.2cm)

Length: 16½" · 26" (41.9 · 66cm)

TOOLS & NOTIONS:

US 8 (5mm) circular needle, 32" and 40" (81.3 and 101.6cm) cords

US J/10–L/11 (6–8mm) crochet hook

(3) 1" (2.5cm) buttons

YARN:

10.5 · 17.5oz (300 · 500g) blow yarn

SWATCHES

Knit 47 · 77 swatches measuring 4¾" x 4¾" (12.1 x 12.1cm). Feel free to use the sample swatches from the projects in the book!

Project	Page for Swatch
Sunset Over the City Sweater	50
Cables and Coffee Sweater	58
Citrus Sweater-Vest	70
Starry Night Cardigan	78
Bring Back the Eighties V-Neck	82
Pink Lemonade Sweater	88
Golden Hour Cardigan	92
Rainbow Picket Fence Sweater	104
Sorbet Date Halter Top	114
Streetwear Sweater	134
Knit-and-Drink Bottle Bag	158
Cotton Candy Handbag	162

CROCHET SWATCHES TOGETHER

Step 1: Place two swatches next to each other.

Step 2: Make a loop on your crochet hook.

Step 3: Insert the crochet hook through the first st on each of your swatches.

Step 4: Pull your thread through the two stitches so that you get 1 new stitch on the crochet hook.

Step 5: Pull the thread through the two stitches on the crochet hook.

Step 6: Repeat Steps 2–4 until the crochet stitches extend the entire length of the swatches.

ASSEMBLY

Lay all the swatches out on your workspace as in the Assembly Diagram. This makes it easier to visualize when you start crocheting the swatches together.

The numbers in the diagram show the order in which the stitches should be crocheted. Start at 1 and work your way up. Start crocheting the swatches together where the number in the illustration is placed, and continue along the zigzag line in the same color as the number.

The swatches get laid out according to the diagram before forming a cardigan.

Crochet the swatches together, as shown in the diagram, for the selected size up to Step 18 · 24. Fold the jacket horizontally along lines 14 · 21 and 16 · 23 so that you get a back piece, two front pieces, and two sleeves. The red zigzag lines show where to crochet together under the sleeves and on the side of the jacket. Complete the rest of the steps in the diagram.

TIP

Knit the 16th stitch in the stitch where you crocheted the swatches together. That way, the transition from the seams and the purl will slide into each other.

HEM

Pick up and knit stitches on the bottom of the jacket with double-thread blow yarn on US 8 (5mm) needle. Knit up 16 sts per test piece = a total of 80 · 144 sts. Work 2" (5.1cm) (K1, P1).

SLEEVES

Pick up stitches along the edge of the sleeve with double-thread blow yarn on US 8 (5mm) needle, 16 sts per swatch = a total of 64 · 64 sts. Knit 1 round while halving the number of stitches as follows: *Knit 2 sts together,* repeat * to * out the row = 32 · 32 sts left on the sleeve.
Work 2" (5.1cm) (K1, P1).

PLACKETS

Knit up stitches along the edge of the jacket with double-thread blow yarn on US 8 (5mm) needle. Knit up 6 sts along both purl boards at the bottom of the jacket and 16 sts per test swatch = a total of 124 · 188 sts. Knit ¾" (1.9cm) purl (K1, 1 vr).
Measure where you want the buttons on the work, so that they get roughly the same distance. Set on a stitch marker on the needle where you want the buttonholes.
Purl up to 1 st before your stitch marker, bind off 1 st. Repeat the number of times you have put on stitch markers for buttonholes.
Purl until where you bind off for buttonholes, cast on 1 st. Repeat the number of times you have put on stitch markers for buttonholes.
Knit until the purl measures approx. 2" (5.1cm) and bind off.
Sew on buttons and secure all threads. Steam or wash the jacket before use.

ASSEMBLY DIAGRAM

Size S

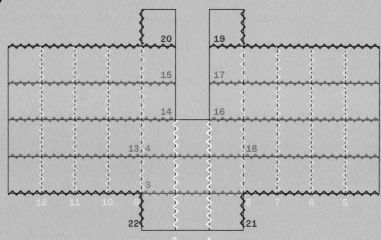

Size L

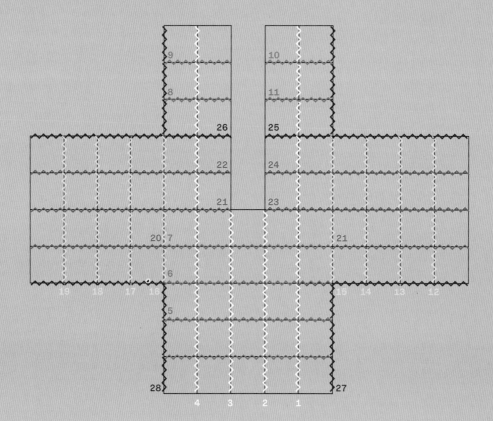

It's so exciting knowing no yarn goes to waste with this cardigan!

Patchwork Tote Bag

#ZWNo10

If you don't have enough swatches to knit an entire cardigan, this tote bag is an easier place to start. It comes in two sizes and is perfect for getting rid of the tiniest scraps that you don't know what to do with. I have knitted the straps for the bag in one color, but these can also be knitted multicolored, with horizontal or vertical stripes, or with a checkerboard pattern.

SIZES: S · L
Width (measured flat): 11½" · 15¾" (29.2 · 40cm)
Length (without handle): 9½" · 14¼" (24.1 · 36.2cm)

TOOLS:
US L/11 (8mm) crochet hook
US 8 (5mm) circular needle, 32" (81.3cm) cord

YARN:
3.5 · 7oz (100 · 200g) thick yarn or double-thread blow yarn

SWATCHES

Knit 8 · 18 swatches measuring 4¾" x 4¾" (12.1 x 12.1cm). Feel free to use the sample swatches for the rest of the projects in the book.

SIDE AND BOTTOM STRIPS

Cast on 8 · 10 sts on US 8 (5mm) needle with a thick wool or mohair yarn or with double-thread blow yarn. Knit stockinette stitch back and forth until the strip measures 9½" · 14¼" (24.1 · 36.2cm). Bind off.

Knit a total of three equal strips. Two will be used for the bag sides and one for the bottom.

ASSEMBLY, STEP 1

Lay out all the swatches as shown in the diagrams on the opposite page.

The numbers in the diagrams show the order in which the stitches should be crocheted. Start at 1 and work your way up. Start crocheting the swatches together where the number in the diagram is placed, and continue along the zigzag line in the same color as the number.

You should now have a grid with 4 · 9 swatches. Make a second grid with the remaining swatches. Crochet the side and bottom strips together as shown in the diagrams.

Size S

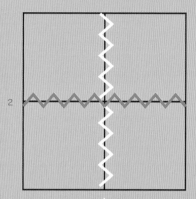

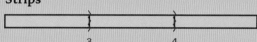

Strips

Size L

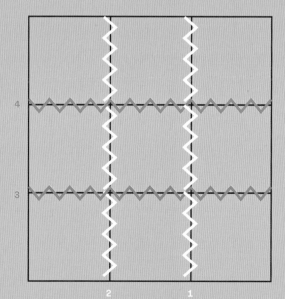

Strips

ASSEMBLY, STEP 2

You will now crochet the strips on the check as follows:

The red lines show where the front of the bag should be crocheted on the strips. The yellow lines show where the back of the bag should be crocheted on the strips. Finish by crocheting a border around the top edge of the bag (the blue line).

HANDLES

Cast on 9 · 13 sts with a thick thread or double-thread blow yarn on US 8 (5mm) needle. Knit double knitting until the handle measures approx. 13½" · 23½" (34.3 · 59.7cm) as follows:

Row 1 (wrong side): *Slip 1 st purl with the thread in front of the work, knit 1 st,* repeat * to * and slip the last st purl off with the thread in front of the work. Turn the work.

Row 2 (right side): *Knit 1 st, slip off 1 st purl with thread in front of the work,* repeat * to * and knit last st. Turn the work.

Sew one end of the first handle to the center of the top-right swatch on the front. Sew the other end to the center of the top-left swatch on the front. Repeat on the back.

Fasten all threads and steam or wash the bag before use.

Size S

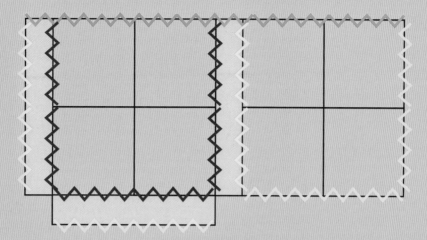

Size L

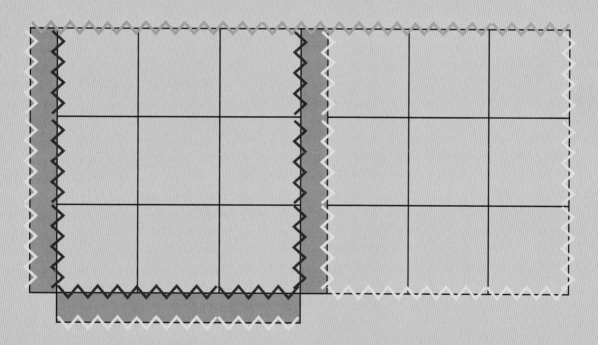

On the Street Collection

Streetwear Sweater

The Streetwear Sweater is one of the first designs I made and a big favorite in my wardrobe. I use it instead of a jacket when it gets colder or when spring announces its arrival, but the air is still cold. It is often used on ski trips; with a windproof jacket underneath, it can be used even on the coldest days.

When I was going to make this in leftover yarn, my yarn stash had started to dwindle, and I was unsure on whether I had enough colors for the whole sweater. Along the way, I decided to switch to a neutral color at the bottom, and I used gradients to make the transition more fluid. The Streetwear Sweater is well suited to both gradients and playing with color, and it can be knitted in all possible color combinations. Unleash your creativity, and I'm sure you'll be left with a sweater that you'll want to walk down the street with.

SIZES: XS · S · M · L · XL
Circumference: 39½" · 42½" · 45½" · 48¾" · 52" (100.3 · 108 · 115.6 · 123.8 · 132.1cm)

Length: 24¾" · 25½" · 26¼" · 27½" · 28¾" (62.9 · 64.8 · 66.7 · 69.9 · 73cm)

GAUGE:
9 sts x 13 rounds = 4" x 4" (10.2 x 10.2cm)

TOOLS:
US 10.5 (6.5mm) circular needle, 16" and 32" (40.6 and 81.3cm) cords

US 10.5 (6.5mm) double-pointed needles

US 10 (6mm) circular needle, 16" and 32" (40.6 and 81.3cm) cords

YARN:
10.5 · 10.5 · 12.5 · 14 · 16oz (300 · 300 · 350 · 400 · 450g) thick mohair yarn

14 · 14 · 17.5 · 19.5 · 21oz (400 · 400 · 500 · 550 · 600g) blow yarn

2.5 · 2.5 · 3.5 · 3.5 · 4.5oz (75 · 75 · 100 · 100 · 125g) thin mohair yarn (can be looped, but gives extra nice color and shape to the sweater)

SAMPLE SWATCH

Cast on 11 sts with two strands of blow yarn and one strand of thick mohair. Knit 16 rows in stockinette stitch, bind off. If the knitting firmness is correct, the swatch should measure approx. 4¾" x 4¾" (12.1 x 12.1cm).

FRONT PIECE LEFT SHOULDER

Cast on 13 · 15 · 16 · 18 · 19 sts with two strands of blow yarn, one strand of thick mohair, and possibly one strand of thin mohair, on US 10 (6mm) circular needle. Knit first purl, then purl 1. On the next needle, the increases start as follows:

Row 1: Knit 1 st, m1r. Knit the rest of the needle.

Row 2: Turn the work over and knit over all P.

Repeat these two rows a total of 4 times. You should now have 17 · 19 · 20 · 22 · 23 sts. Cut the thread and start on the right shoulder while the left shoulder rests on the needle.

FRONT PIECE RIGHT SHOULDER

Cast on 13 · 15 · 16 · 18 · 19 sts on US 10 (6mm) circular needle and knit the first needle in the right. Then knit 1 row in the right. On the next needle, begin the increases in the same way as on the left shoulder, but on the other side of the needle like this:

Row 1: K until 1 st remains on the needle, inc. Knit the last st and turn the piece.

Row 2: K over all sts.

Repeat these two rows a total of 4 times. You should now have 17 · 19 · 20 · 22 · 23 sts on both the right and left shoulder. The next needle starts on the right side on the right shoulder.

FRONT PIECE

Knit over the stitches of the right shoulder, cast on 10 · 10 · 12 · 12 · 13 sts on the needle, knit over the left shoulder stitches.

You have now joined the two shoulders and should have 44 · 48 · 52 · 56 · 59 sts on the front piece. Continue stockinette stitch until the front piece measures 12½" · 13½" · 14¼" · 15" · 15¾" (31.8 · 34.3 · 36.2 · 38.1 · 40cm) from the shoulder down, and finish so that the next row to be knitted is on the right side.

Cut the thread and transfer the front piece's stitches onto a stitch holder or cord. You will now start on the back piece.

RIGHT SHOULDER BACK PIECE

Pick up and knit 13 · 15 · 16 · 18 · 19 sts with US 10 (6mm) circular needle on the right side between the stitches on the right shoulder. Work the next row purl. Furthermore, you should increase to the neck as follows:

Row 1: Knit 1 sl st, m1r, knit the rest of the row.

Row 2: Turn the work over and knit over all P.

Repeat these two rows a total of 2 times until you have 15 · 17 · 18 · 20 · 21 sts. Cut the thread and place stiches on hold on the needle while you start on the left shoulder.

LEFT SHOULDER BACK PIECE

Pick up and knit 13 · 15 · 16 · 18 · 19 sts on the right side between the stitches on the left shoulder on US 10 (6mm) circular needle. Purl the next row. Then increase to neck like this:

Row 1: K until 1 st remains on the needle, inc. Knit the last st and turn the piece.

I wear this sweater in early spring and late fall as well as winter. If you have a specific season in mind, you may want to pick colors to match!

I love the high turtleneck on this sweater because it covers my neck until my hairline, keeping me nice and warm!

Row 2: K over all sts.

Repeat these two rows a total of 2 times, until you have 15 · 17 · 18 · 20 · 21 sts on the row and the next row should be knitted from the right side.

BACK PIECE

K over all sts on the left shoulder, cast on 14 · 14 · 16 · 16 · 17 sts on the needle, K over all sts on the right shoulder.

You have now joined the two shoulders and have 44 · 48 · 52 · 56 · 59 sts on the back piece. Knit in stockinette stitch until the back piece measures 12 ½" · 13½" · 14¼" · 15" · 15¾" (31.8 · 34.3 · 36.2 · 38.1 · 40cm) and finish with a purl row so that the next row is knitted from the right side.

You will now join the back piece and the front piece and start knitting in the round.

TORSO

K over all sts on the back piece, cast on 1 st. Put the stitches of the front piece back on the needle and knit over the stitches of the front piece. Cast on 1 st and insert a stitch marker to mark the beginning of the round.

You now have 90 · 98 · 106 · 114 · 120 sts on the torso. Knit in stockinette stitch until the piece measures 22¾" · 24½" · 25¼" · 26¼" · 27½" (57.8 · 62.2 · 64.1 · 66.7 · 69.9cm) or the desired length.

Bind off 4 · 4 · 6 · 6 · 8 sts on the next round so you have 86 · 94 · 100 · 108 · 112 sts and change to US 10.5 (6.5mm) needle. Work 3" (7.6cm) (K1, P1) rib and bind off. For best result, the Italian bind-off is recommended.

SLEEVES

Pick up and knit 52 · 56 · 60 · 64 · 68 sts with US 10 (6mm) circular needle for sleeves evenly distributed on the front piece and the back piece (25 · 28 · 30 · 32 · 34 sts each side). Start under the sleeve for the finest transition.

Work in stockinette stitch until the sleeve measures 11¾" · 12½" · 13½" · 14¼" · 14¼" (29.8 · 31.8 · 34.3 · 36.2 · 36.2cm) or desired length.

Furthermore, 6 · 7 · 7 · 8 · 8 sts must be reduced every 3rd round on the sleeve as follows:

Round 1: Bind off 6 · 7 · 7 · 8 · 8 sts evenly distributed over the round.

Round 2: K over all sts.

Round 3: K over all sts.

Repeat these three rows a total of 4 times. If necessary, switch to double-pointed needles before dec 10 · 8 · 12 · 10 · 14 sts on the next round. You should now have 18 · 20 · 20 · 22 · 22 sts. Change to US 10.5 (6.5mm) circular or double-pointed needles, and work 3" (7.6cm) (K1, P1) rib. Bind off with Italian tubular bind off.

Knit a similar sleeve on the other side.

NECK

Pick up and knit 46 · 46 · 50 · 50 · 52 sts on US 10.5 (6.5mm) circular needle for neck, evenly spaced. Start between the transition from the right shoulder and the back piece. Work 5½" (14cm) (K1, P1) rib, bind off with Italian tubular bind off. Sew the neck down or leave it as is.

Tie off all loose threads. Steam or wash the sweater so that the edges where you have knitted up stitches for the neck and sleeves become less visible.

Butter Brioche Scarf

The zero-waste collection needed a quick-knit, chunky, and delicious scarf, and then there was no doubt that brk was the way to go. With a brioche pattern, the scarf is the same on both sides, at the same time being suitable for combining different colors. The scarf can easily be knitted longer than stated if you have a lot of yarn to spare.

SIZE:
Width: 7¾" (19.7cm)
Length: 73" (185.4cm)

GAUGE:
9 sts x 14 rounds in stockinette stitch = 4" x 4" (10.2 x 10.2cm)

TOOLS:
US 10 (6mm) circular needle, 32" (81.3cm) cords

YARN:
4.5oz (125g) thick mohair yarn
8oz (225g) blow yarn

This chunky scarf is not only cute but also great for those cold winter days.

Cast on 17 sts on US 10 (6mm) circular needle with two strands of blow yarn and one strand of thick mohair. Work brioche pattern as follows:

Row 1 (wrong side): Slip 1 st purl off the needle with the thread in front of the work (edge stitch). *Knit 1 st, yarn over, and slip the next stitch purl off.* Repeat * to * until there are 2 sts left on the needle. Knit these two sts.

Row 2 (right side): Slip 1 st purl off the needle with the thread in front of the work (edge stitch). *Yarn over, and slip 1 st purl, knit 1 sl st (brk),* repeat * to * until there are 2 sts left on the needle. Yarn over, and slip 1 st purl, knit 1 sl st (edge stitch).

Row 3 (wrong side): Slip 1 st purl off the needle with the thread in front of the work (edge stitch). *Knit 1 brk, yarn over, and slip 1 st purl off,* repeat * to * until there are 3 sts left on the needle. Yarn over, and slip 1 st purl, knit 1 brk, knit 1 sl st (edge stitch).

Continue in stockinette stitch by repeating Rows 2–3 until the piece measures approx. 73" (185.4cm) or desired length. The scarf can be knitted longer if you have more yarn to spare.

Bind off with straight stitches.

Sew or crochet in all threads.

To add a fringe to the ends of your scarf, follow the steps on the opposite page.

Making the Fringe

Step 1: Cut up threads approx. 12" (30.5cm) long. Join 3 strands per stitch at each end of the scarf.

Step 2: Using a crochet hook, take it through the first stitch at the end of the scarf.

Step 3: Pick up 3 threads with the crochet hook in the middle of the threads and pull through the first stitch so that you get a loop.

Step 4: Pull the rest of the yarn through this loop and tighten.

Step 5: Repeat in all the stitches on both ends of the scarf.

Painted Desert Sweater

This V-neck is another beloved addition to the On the Street collection. This was the last leftover yarn sweater I knitted in this book, and since my yarn stash was already quite thin, I had to be a little creative to get enough yarn for the whole garment. I picked up small and larger projects I had lying around, and was left with a pile of skeins in various sizes and colors.

I found that the easiest method would be to knit with a play of colors without a base color, trying my hand at different colors and types of yarn. To sew it all together, I chose to knit the purl rows in one color that I had a lot of: a vibrant yellow color. This sweater is a properly recycled leftover piece and a nice end to the big leftover yarn projects.

SIZES: XS · S · M · L · XL

Circumference: 20" · 22" · 23½" · 25¼" · 26¾" (50.8 · 55.8 · 59.7 · 64.1 · 67.9cm)

Length: 20½" · 22" · 23½" · 25½" · 26¾" (52.1 · 55.8 · 59.7 · 64.1 · 67.9cm)

Sleeve length: 14½" · 15" · 16½" · 18" · 19½" (36.2 · 38.1 · 41.9 · 45.7 · 49.5cm)

GAUGE:

9 sts x 13 rows = 4" (10.2cm)

TOOLS:

US 10 (6mm) circular needle, 16" and 32" (40.6 and 81.3cm) cords

US 11 (8mm) circular needle, 16" and 32" (40.6 and 81.3cm) cords, possibly double-pointed needles

YARN:

9 · 10.5 · 12.5 · 14 · 16oz (250 · 300 · 350 · 400 · 450g) thick mohair yarn

14 · 14 · 17.5 · 19.5 · 21oz (400 · 400 · 500 · 550 · 600g) double-thread blow yarn or 21 · 23 · 28.25 · 31.75 · 33.5oz (600 · 650 · 800 · 900 · 950g) thick yarn

SAMPLE SWATCH

Cast on 11 sts with two strands of blow yarn and one strand of thick mohair. Knit 16 rows in stockinette stitch, bind off. If the knitting firmness is correct, the swatch should measure approx. 4¾" x 4¾" (12.1 x 12.1cm).

LEFT SHOULDER FRONT PIECE

Cast on 14 · 15 · 17 · 18 · 20 sts on US 10 (6mm) needle for the left shoulder. Work 1 purl row. On the next row, start increasing to a V-neck like this:

Row 1: Knit 1 st, inc. Knit the rest of the needle.

Row 2: Turn the work and purl over all sts.

Row 3: Knit all sts.

Row 4: Purl all sts.

Repeat these 4 rows a total of 8 · 9 · 9 · 10 · 10 times until you have 22 · 24 · 26 · 28 · 30 sts. Cut the thread and place stiches on hold on the needle. You will now start on the right shoulder.

RIGHT SHOULDER FRONT PIECE

Cast on 14 · 15 · 17 · 18 · 20 sts on US 10 (6mm) needle for the right shoulder. Work 1 row purl. On the next needle, start increasing to a V-neck like this:

Row 1: K until 1 st remains on the needle. M1l. Knit the last st on the needle.

Row 2: Turn the work and purl over all sts.

Row 3: Knit all sts.

Row 4: Purl all sts.

Repeat these 4 rows a total of 8 · 9 · 9 · 10 · 10 times until you have 22 · 24 · 26 · 28 · 30 sts. The next row is from the right side. You will now unite the two shoulders into one assembled front piece.

FRONT PIECE

K over all the stitches on the right shoulder. Place 1 st on the needle (this stitch marks the middle of the V-neck) and knit over the stitches of the left shoulder. You now have 45 · 49 · 53 · 57 · 61 sts on the front piece.

Knit until the front piece measures 11¾" · 13½" · 15" · 16½" · 18" (29.8 · 34.3 · 38.1 · 41.9 · 45.7cm) from the shoulder down. Finish with a purl row so that the next row is knitted from the right side. Cut the thread and transfer the stitches onto a stitch holder or thread.

RIGHT SHOULDER BACK PIECE

Pick up and knit 14 · 15 · 17 · 18 · 20 sts on US 10 (6mm) needle between the already existing stitches on the right shoulder of the front piece. Purl 1 row. Furthermore, you should increase to the neck as follows:

Row 1: Knit 1 st, inc. Knit the rest of the row.

Row 2: Turn the work over and purl.

Row 3: Knit all sts.

Row 4: Purl all sts.

Repeat these 4 rows a total of 2 times until you have 16 · 17 · 19 · 20 · 22 sts on the needle. Cut the thread and leave the stitches to rest on the needle while you knit the left shoulder.

LEFT SHOULDER BACK PIECE

Pick up and knit 14 · 15 · 17 · 18 · 20 sts on US 10 (6mm) needle between the already existing stitches on the left shoulder of the front piece. Purl 1 row. Furthermore, you should increase to the neck as follows:

Row 1: K until 1 st remains on the needle. M1l. Knit the last st on the needle.

Row 2: Turn the work over and purl 1 row.

Row 3: Knit all sts.

Row 4: Purl all sts.

Repeat these 4 rows a total of 2 times until you have 16 · 17 · 19 · 20 · 22 sts on the needle. The next row is knitted from the right side.

BACK PIECE

K over all the stitches on the right shoulder of the back piece. Cast on 13 · 15 · 15 · 17 · 17 sts on the needle and knit over the stitches of the left shoulder on the back piece. You now have 45 · 49 · 53 · 57 · 61 sts on the back piece.

Continue in stockinette stitch until the piece measures 11¾" · 13½" · 15" · 16½" · 18" (29.8 · 34.3 · 38.1 · 41.9 · 45.7cm) from the shoulder down. Finish with a purl stitch so that the next stitch is knitted from the right side. You should now have a front piece and a back piece that are the same length, and in the next round you should join the two parts to the torso.

TORSO

K over the stitches on the back piece, cast on 1 st, K over the stitches on the front piece, cast on 1 st. Insert a stitch marker to mark the beginning of the round. You have now joined the front piece and the back piece and should have 92 · 100 · 108 · 116 · 124 sts. Continue to knit in stockinette stitch until the piece measures 21¼" · 22¾" · 24½" · 26" · 27½" (54 ·

The length will contract somewhat when you knit up stitches for the sleeve, so the sweater will be somewhat shorter in the end.

57.8 · 62.2 · 66 · 69.9cm) measured from the shoulder down.

Change to US 8 (5mm) needle and work 2" (5.1cm) (K1, P1). Bind off.

SLEEVES

Pick up and knit 48 · 52 · 56 · 60 · 64 sts for sleeve on US 10 (6mm) needle. Make sure the stitches are evenly distributed between the front piece and the back piece (24 · 26 · 28 · 30 · 32 sts on each side). You should continue to knit in stockinette stitch, without increasing or decreasing stitches, until the sleeve measures 15" · 15¾" · 16½" · 17½" · 18" (38.1 · 40 · 41.9 · 44.4 · 45.7cm) or the desired length. Feel free to try the sweater on along the way. On the next round, you will halve the sleeve stitch count as follows:

Knit 2 sts together, repeat from * to * until you have 24 · 26 · 28 · 30 · 32 sts left. Change to US 8 (5mm) needle and work 2" (5.1cm) (K1, P1). Bind off.

Knit a corresponding sleeve in the same way.

NECK

Pick up and knit 80 · 86 · 86 · 92 · 92 sts for the neck on US 8 (5mm) needle. Start at the back piece and distribute the stitches as follows: 13 · 15 · 15 · 17 · 17 sts in the middle of the back piece, 8 sts on the left shoulder of the back piece, 25 · 27 · 27 · 29 · 29 sts on each side of the V on the front piece, 1 st in the middle in the front marking the center of the V-neck, 8 sts on the right shoulder of the back piece.

Work (K1, P1) until 1 st before the middle stitch in the center of the V-neck, slip 2 sts together off the needle as if you had knit them together. Knit the next st, and pull the 2 sts you slipped off the needle over the stitch you just knitted. This way, you form the V with your middle stitch centered.

Continue to knit like this with decs for a V-neck every round, until the rib measures 2" (5.1cm) from the neck.

Bind off and fasten all loose threads. Steam or wash the sweater, then the edges where you have knitted up stitches for the neck and sleeves will also become less visible.

RIGHT: V-neck sweaters have always felt more versatile because you can wear them alone or with a shirt underneath. This could be a staple of your wardrobe for years!

Streetwear Mittens

Here are a pair of delightful, thick mittens that are perfect for cold winter days. These are knitted in the same yarn combination as the rest of the On the Street collection and can easily be matched with the Streetwear Sweater. The mittens are also quickly knitted and are suitable as gifts. The dense knitting makes them nice and cozy, keeping your hands warm even on the coldest winter days.

SIZES: S · M · L

Width: 3½" · 4" · 4⅓" (8.9 · 10.2 · 11cm)

Length: 9¾" · 10¼" · 10½" (24.8 · 26 · 26.7cm)

GAUGE:

12 sts x 20 rounds in stockinette stitch on US 10.5 (6.5mm) = 4" x 4" (10.2 x 10.2cm)

TOOLS:

US 10.5 (6.5mm) double-pointed needles (or circular needles if using the magic loop technique)

US 10 (6mm) double-pointed needles (or circular needles if using the magic loop technique)

YARN:

1.75 · 2.25 · 2.75oz (50 · 65 · 75g) blow yarn

1.25 · 1.4 · 1.6oz (35 · 40 · 45g) thick mohair yarn

Cast on 18 · 20 · 22 sts on US 10 (6mm) double-pointed needles with one strand of thick mohair and two strands of blow yarn.

Work 3" (7.6cm) (K1, P1) rib.

Switch to US 10.5 (6.5mm) needle and knit 1 round while increasing 4 sts evenly distributed = 22 · 24 · 26 sts on the needle. If you knit with the magic loop technique, you can insert a stitch marker at the beginning of the round and one after 11 · 12 · 13 sts to mark the front and back of the mitten. Furthermore, it must be increased to a thumb; the increases are made the same for all sizes.

RIGHT THUMB OPENING

Round 1: Knit 2 sts, m1r, knit 1 st, inc K. Knit the round.

Round 2: K without increasing.

Round 3: Knit 2 sts, m1r, knit 3 sts, inc K. Knit the r out the round.

Round 4: K without increasing.

Continue knitting until the piece measures 5" · 5½" · 6" (12.7 · 14 · 15.2cm). On in the next round, bind off stitches for the thumb like this:

Knit 1 · 1 · 1 st, bind off 7 · 7 · 7 sts on a knitting needle or a thread, cast on 3 · 3 · 3 sts with a loop arrangement on the needle, and knit the round.

LEFT THUMB OPENING

Round 1: Knit 8 · 9 · 10 sts, m1r, knit 1 st, m1l. Knit the round.

Round 2: K without increasing.

Round 3: Knit 8 · 9 · 10 sts, m1r, work 3 sts, m1l. Knit the round.

Round 4: K without increasing.

Continue knitting until the piece measures 5" · 5½" · 6" (12.7 · 14 · 15.2cm). On in the next round, bind off stitches for the thumb like this:

Knit 7 · 8 · 9 sts, bind off 7 · 7 · 7 sts on a knitting needle or thread, cast on 3 · 3 · 3 sts with a loop arrangement on the needle, and continue to knit the round.

Knit until hand piece measures 9½" · 9½" · 9½" (24.1 · 24.1 · 24.1cm).

Furthermore, bind off stitches in a V shape at the top of the mitten.

Magic Loop

Ssk, knit until 2 sts before your stitch marker, k2tog, slip the stitch marker over to the right needle, ssk. Knit until there are 2 sts left on the needle, k2tog = 4 sts bind off.

Double-Pointed Needles

Distribute the stitches so that you have 5 · 6 · 6 sts on the first needle, 6 · 6 · 7 sts on the second needle, 5 · 6 · 6 sts on the third needle, and 6 · 6 · 7 sts on the fourth needle. Ssk at the beginning of the first needle, knit until there are 2 sts left on the second needle, k2tog, ssk at the beginning of the third needle, work until there are 2 sts left on the round, k2tog = 4 sts.

The decreases are repeated as follows for the different sizes:

Size S and L

Repeat the dec every round until there are 6 sts left on the needle. *Slip the first stitch on the right needle, knit 2 sts together, slip the first stitch on the right needle over the second stitch* = 2 sts. Repeat * to *. Cut the thread and pull it through the 2 remaining stitches.

Size M

Repeat the decreases every round until there are 4 sts left on the needle, change the thread, and pull it through the 4 stitches.

THUMB

The thumb is knitted the same for all three sizes. Put the 7 sts you left off for the thumb back on the needle. You must also pick up stitches as follows: Pick up 1 st between the stitches on the needle and the back of the mitten; pick up 3 sts from the back of the mitten and 1 st between the back of the mitten and the stitches on the needle = 12 sts. Distribute the stitches on the double needle so that you have 3 sts on each of the needles. If you knit with the magic loop technique, you can put on a starting marker at the beginning of the round and one after 6 sts.

Knit until the thumb measures 2⅛" · 2⅓" · 2½" (5.4 · 5.9 · 6.4cm) or desired length measured from where you picked up stitches. Feel free to try the mitten on along the way. Furthermore, you must decrease to the thumb in the same way as on the mitten itself:

Magic Loop

Ssk, knit until 2 sts before your stitch marker, k2tog, slip the stitch marker over to the right needle, ssk. Knit until there are 2 sts left on the round, k2tog = 4 decreases.

Double-Pointed Needles

Ssk at the beginning of the first needle, knit until 2 sts remain on your second needle, k2tog, ssk at the beginning of the third needle, knit until 2 sts remain on the round, k2tog = 4 sts.

Repeat the decreases until there are 4 sts left on the needle, change the thread, and pull it through the 4 decreases.

Fasten all loose threads and wash the mittens before using them.

Streetwear Bucket Hat

This thick bucket hat is knitted in the same yarn combination as the rest of the On the Street collection and can easily be matched with the Streetwear Sweater and Mittens. It is a perfect leftover yarn project and a stylish, warming accessory.

SIZES: S · M · L

Circumference: 19" · 21¼" · 23½" (48.3 · 54 · 59.7cm)

GAUGE:

12 sts x 20 rounds in stockinette stitch on US 10.5 (6.5mm) = 4" x 4" (10.2 x 10.2cm)

TOOLS:

US 10.5 (6.5mm) circular needle, 16" (40.6cm) cords

US 10.5 (6.5mm) double-pointed needles (if you prefer using dpn for the magic loop technique)

YARN:

1.6 · 1.75 · 2oz (45 · 50 · 60g) blow yarn

1 · 1.25 · 1.4oz (30 · 35 · 40g) thick mohair yarn

The hat is divided into three parts: top, body, and brim. The top is knitted using the magic loop technique while increasing 8 stitches every other round. The hat is then knitted in the round without increasing until the stated or desired length, before the edge is knitted by continuing to increase every third round in the same way as on the top of the hat.

Cast on 8 · 8 · 8 sts with two strands of blow yarn and one strand of thick mohair on US 10.5 (6.5mm) circular needle, 15¾" (40cm); if you prefer to use double-pointed needles, you can cast on stitches on US 10.5 (6.5mm) double-pointed needles and switch to circular needles when the number of stitches allows it.

Furthermore, you will knit with the magic loop technique like this:

Move the stitches over to the left needle, so that the thread of the work is on the back stitch on the needle. Knit the first stitch on the needle while tightening so that the front and back stitches meet, and the piece is worked in the round. Knit the rest of the stitches on the needle, make sure to knit tightly on the first stitches.

This part can be a little tricky but gets better once you start increasing stitches.

Continue knitting in the round with the magic loop technique while increasing sts as follows:

Round 1: *Knit 1 st, cast on 1 st with a loop pattern,* repeat from * to * out the row = 8 sts increased.

Round 2: Knit all the stitches, including the stitches you added on the previous round.

Round 3: *Knit 2 sts, cast on 1 st with a loop pattern,* repeat from * to * out the row = 8 sts increased.

Round 4: Knit all the stitches, including the stitches you cast on in the previous round.

Continue to increase 8 sts every other round by adding 1 st to the stitches knitted before each increase for each round. Increase a total of 6 · 7 · 8 times = 56 · 64 · 72 sts on the needle.

Knit without increasing until the piece measures 2¾" · 2¾" · 2¾" (7 · 7 · 7cm) or the desired length, measured from the last round you increased, and down.

Furthermore, you must increase to the edge of the hat as follows:

Round 1: *Knit 7 · 8 · 9 sts, cast on 1 st with a loop pattern,* repeat from * to * out the row.

Round 2: K.

Round 3: K.

Continue to increase 8 sts every third round by adding 1 st on the stitches knitted before each increase. Increase a total of 4 · 4 · 4 times = 88 · 96 · 104 sts on the needle. Bind off.

Fasten all loose threads and wash the hat before use. To prevent the brim of the hat from curling, you can try laying the hat flat under pressure (for example, a stack of books or something else heavy).

RIGHT: The three Streetwear pieces were made to go together, but you can pair the accessories with another sweater or make them completely unique.

Knit-and-Drink Bottle Bag

I have seen this bottle bag countless times in a crocheted version, and I have always wanted one. I'm not very good at crocheting, so I decided to knit it instead. The bag is perfect for taking to the park, to your next knitting and drinking event, or on a trip with a water bottle.

In addition, it is also the perfect accessory if you are giving a bottle of wine as a gift. The project is based on thick cotton, but this can just as well be knitted in double-thread cotton yarn or triple-thread thin cotton—just remember to check the gauge.

SIZE:

Length (measured flat without handle): 9½" (24.1cm)

Width (measured flat): 4¾" (12.1cm)

GAUGE:

16 sts x 25 rounds in stockinette stitch = 4" x 4" (10.2 x 10.2cm)

TOOLS:

US 7 (4.5mm) circular needle

YARN:

2.75oz (75g) thick cotton yarn

NOTE The mesh pattern and handle will stretch when a heavy bottle is inserted. Feel free to check that the length is what you want along the way, and make the necessary adjustments.

SAMPLE SWATCH

Cast on 20 sts. Knit in stockinette stitch until the swatch measures 4¾" (12.1cm). If the knitting tension is correct, the swatch should measure approx. 4¾" x 4¾" (12.1 x 12.1cm).

BOTTOM

Cast on 8 · 8 · 8 sts with a thread of thick cotton on US 7 (4.5mm) circular needle. If you prefer to use dpn, you can cast on stitches on US 10.5 (6.5mm) double-pointed needle and switch to circular needle when the number of stitches allows. Furthermore, you will knit with the magic loop technique like this:

Move the stitches over to the left side so that the thread of the work is on the back stitch on the needle. Knit the first stitch on the needle while tightening so that the front and back stitches meet and the piece is worked in the round. Knit the rest of the stitches on the needle, making sure to knit tightly on the first stitches.

This part can be a little tricky but gets better once you start increasing stitches.

Continue knitting in the round with the magic loop technique while increasing sts as follows:

Round 1: *Knit 1 st, cast on 1 st with a loop pattern,* repeat from * to * out the row = 8 sts increased.

Round 2: Knit all the stitches, including the stitches you cast on in the previous round.

Round 3: *Knit 2 sts, cast on 1 st with a loop pattern,* repeat * to * out the row = 8 sts increased.

Round 4: Knit all the stitches, including the stitches you cast on in the previous round.

Continue to increase 8 sts every other round by adding 1 st to the stitches knitted before each increase for each round. Increase a total of 4 times = 40 sts on the needle. Knit in the round for approx. 1" (2.5cm) from where you last increased.

MESH PATTERN

Furthermore, you must work the lace pattern back and forth as follows:

Row 1 (right side): Slip 1 st purl off the needle, *knit 2 sts together, knit 1 yarn over ,* repeat * to * until 2 sts remain, knit 2 sts.

Row 2 (wrong side): Slip 1 stitch K off the needle, purl until 1 st remains, knit 1 st.

Row 3: Slip 1 st from needle, knit 1 st. *Knit 2 sts together, knit 1 yarn over,* repeat * to * until 1 st remains, knit 1 st.

TIP

Do you want a wider bag for a prosecco bottle, or perhaps even bigger to be used as a project bag, you can continue to increase stitches on the bottom until you reach the desired circumference. The mesh pattern is worked as indicated with your new stitch count. When you bind off stitches for the string at the top of the bag, divide your stitch count by 2 and subtract 8 sts (1 st into each of the holes and 6 sts between) to center the holes on the front of the bag. Voilà! You have your own bag in the desired width!

Row 4: Repeat Row 2.

Repeat Rows 1–4 until the mesh pattern measures approx. 6¼" (15.9cm) or desired length.

TOP EDGE

On the next round, you should start knitting in the round again to the drawstring edge of the bag. Two holes must be cut for tying the cords before the edge is knitted or sewn down. Knit 3 rounds K. Knit 16 sts, bind off 1 st, knit 6 sts, bind off 1 st, knit 16 sts.

Knit 16 sts, cast on 1 st with a loop, knit 6 sts, cast on 1 st with a loop, knit 16 sts. Knit 5 rounds K. Knit the edge down as you bind off, or bind off and sew the edge down.

Finger knit a string approx. 25½"–27½" (64.8–69.9cm) long or desired length. Thread the string through the edge of the bag using a safety pin. Sew the back of the bag together.

HANDLE

Cast on 6 sts on US 7 (4.5mm) needle. Use the i-cord technique, and knit in the round until the handle measures approx. 31½" (80cm) or desired length. Knit like this:

Move the stitches over to the left needle so that the thread of the work is on the back stitch on the needle. Knit the first stitch on the needle while tightening, so that the front and back stitches meet and the piece is worked in the round. Knit the rest of the stitches on the needle, making sure to knit tightly on the first stitches.

Sew the handle on the bag.

This bag can be used for wine bottles, but it is also perfect for water bottles as well.

Cotton Candy Handbag

This bag is the perfect project for your cotton yarn. It is knitted with three threads of cotton in different colors, which gives it a nice play of color, but can also be knitted in one color. You need two round handles for the bag; these can be purchased at some knitting shops and hobby shops. But if you, like me, don't have round handles available, they can also be easily knitted. Use old scraps of yarn as filling for the handles, and you really get to use up your leftovers.

SIZE:
Width (measured flat): 12½" (31.8cm)
Length: 7¾" (19.7cm)

GAUGE:
17 sts x 26 rounds in stockinette stitch on US 6
   (4mm) = 4" x 4" (10.2 x 10.2cm)

TOOLS:
US 6 (4mm) circular needle, 24" (61cm) cords

YARN:
Color 1: 3.5oz (100g) cotton yarn
Color 2: 3.5oz (100g) cotton yarn
1.8oz (50g) thin cotton yarn

SAMPLE SWATCH

Cast on 20 sts. Knit 31 rows in stockinette stitch. If the gauge is correct, the sample swatch should measure 4¾" x 4¾" (12.1 x 12.1cm).

BOTTOM

Cast on US 6 (4mm) needle with Judy's Magic Cast On, 24 sts on each needle, so that you have a total of 48 sts spread over 2 needles.

Start with the top needle. Knit 6 rows in stockinette stitch. Cut the thread.

Continue with the bottom needle, knitting 6 rows in stockinette stitch.

You will now start knitting in the round.

BAG

Pick up 10 sts along the edge of the bottom, knit over the first needle. Pick up 10 sts along the bottom and knit out the next needle. You now have 68 sts on the needle. Insert a stitch marker at the start of the round, after 10 sts, after 34 sts and after 44 sts.

Put on a start marker. Knit 11 sts, inc, insert a stitch marker. Knit 22 sts, insert a stitch marker, inc. Knit 12 sts, inc, insert a stitch marker. Knit 22 sts, insert a stitch marker, inc, knit 1 st = 4 sts increased.

K 1 round without increasing. Furthermore, you must continue to increase 4 sts every other round as follows:

Round 1: *Knit until the stitch marker, m1r. Knit until your next stitch marker, slip the marker onto the right needle, m1l,* repeat * to *. Knit the round.

Round 2: K without increasing.

Repeat Rounds 1 and 2 a total of 9 times = 108 sts on the needle.

Knit in rows until the piece measures approx. 7¾" (19.7cm), measured flat on the center of the bag. Cut the thread.

Insert new yarn at the last stitch marker before your starting marker. Knit 32 sts double knitting like this:

Row 1 (right side): *Knit 1 st, slip 1 st purl off with the thread in front of the work,* repeat * to * until you have worked a total of 32 sts double knitting.

Row 2 (wrong side): Turn the piece. *Knit 1 st, slip 1 st purl off with the thread in front of the work,* repeat * to * until you have knitted a total of 32 sts double knit.

Turn the work to the right side again and bind off 32 sts with straight stitches.

Knit the next 22 sts and place stiches on hold.

Knit double over the next 32 sts:

Row 1 (right side): *Knit 1 st, slip 1 st purl off with the thread in front of the work,* repeat * to * until you have worked a total of 32 sts double knitting.

Row 2 (wrong side): Turn the piece. *Knit 1 st, slip 1 st purl off with the thread in front of the work,* repeat * to * until you have knitted a total of 32 sts double knit.

Turn the work to the right side again and bind off 32 sts with straight stitches.

K over the next 22 sts, turn the work, and K back. Continue back and forth like this until the piece measures approx. 2½" (6.4cm). Cut off and cut the thread.

Add new yarn to the right side of the last 22 stitches on the needle, K over the next 22 sts. Continue back and forth in stockinette stitch until the piece measures approx. 2½" (6.4cm). Bind off.

HANDLES

Round handles can be bought at some yarn shops and hobby shops, or you can knit them yourself, as I have done here.

Cast on 6 sts. Knit in the round with the i-cord technique until the handle measures approx. 13¾" (34.9cm). Fill the void in the handle with old yarn scraps, cotton or similar.

Sew together the beginning and end of the strip you have knitted, so you get a round handle.

ASSEMBLY

Place a handle on the strip with 22 sts on one side of the bag. Fold the strip over the handle and sew/crochet down. Repeat with the other handle on the other side of the bag.

Fasten all threads.

A label can be for your business, but it can also be used for telling your loved ones that this gift came from you!

Index

Note: Page numbers in *italics* indicate projects.

Thank You Very Much

A dream has come true, and what an adventure this project has been! Many thanks to Kagge Forlag and my editor Solveig Øye, who had faith in me and my project. It has been an honor to work with you, and I am eternally grateful for the opportunity. Many thanks to all contributors to the book: Thanks to photographer Guro Sommer, who was a dream to work with. You gave the pictures in the book a unique playfulness and provided good input and advice along the way, which I greatly appreciated. Thanks to Trine + Kim for a fantastic job with the book's graphic design. I also have to thank my test knitters who have knitted and quality assured the patterns in this book. Without their feedback and input, the patterns would not have been of the same high standard.

Many thanks to my dear partner Isak who has put up with the chaos that comes with knitting 20 leftover yarn projects. You have stuck by me when I have been stressed and have been a supporter throughout the project. Thank you for being patient, generous, and committed to everything I do.

This book would also not have been possible without support from my family. Thanks to mom and dad, who always pitch in, who help with projects, and who support me no matter what. Also, thanks to my older brother Ulrik for both good and motivating conversations along the way.

Thank you to all the friends who support, inspire, and cheer me on, and who were ready to welcome me when I came out of my sometimes isolating writing bubble. You are worth gold.

Finally, I have to thank the person who started it all: my grandmother, Evelyn. She sat patiently

and taught me the basic knitting techniques, and she framed my very first little knitwear. Thank you very much for giving me an interest in knitting and for always being committed, caring, and supportive.